David Rudovsky practices law in Philadelphia and is Staff Counsel for the National Emergency Civil Liberties Committee. He has been counsel in many cases involving prisoners' rights and is currently representing inmates of the Philadelphia County Prison System in a court action seeking improvement of prison conditions. Mr. Rudovsky teaches at the University of Pennsylvania School of Law and is the co-author of *Police Misconduct: Law and Litigation*.

Alvin J. Bronstein and **Edward I. Koren** are the Executive Director and a Staff Attorney, respectively, of the National Prison Project of the ACLU Foundation. The National Prison Project is a tax-exempt foundation funded project which seeks to broaden prisoners' rights, to improve overall prison conditions by using administrative, legislative, and judicial channels, and to develop alternatives to incarceration.

Julia D. Cade is a paralegal and public information assistant for the National Prison Project of the ACLU in Washington. She has recently joined the Prison Project staff after many years in Georgia working on various death penalty and prison issues.

D1560291

Also in this series

AN AMERICAN CIVIL LIBERTIES UNION HANDBOOK

THE RIGHTS OF PRISONERS

THE BASIC ACLU GUIDE TO PRISONERS' RIGHTS

FOURTH EDITION

**David Rudovsky
Alvin J. Bronstein
Edward I. Koren
Julia D. Cade**

General Editor of the Handbook Series:
Norman Dorsen, President, ACLU

SOUTHERN ILLINOIS UNIVERSITY PRESS
CARBONDALE AND EDWARDSVILLE

Copyright © 1988 by the American Civil Liberties Union
All rights reserved
Printed in the United States of America
Edited by Sally Master
Production supervised by Natalia Nadraga

91 90 89   4 3

Library of Congress Cataloging-in-Publication Data

Rudovsky, David.
  The rights of prisoners.

  (An American Civil Liberties Union handbook)
  1. Prisoners—Legal status, laws, etc.—
United States. I. Bronstein, Alvin J. II. Koren,
Edward I. III. Cade, Julia D. IV. Title. V. Series.
KF9731.Z9R8 1988   344.73′035643   87-23577
ISBN 0-8093-1452-5   347.30435643

The paper used in this publication meets the minimum requirements of
American National Standard for Information Sciences—Permanence of
Paper for Printed Library Materials, ANSI Z39.48-1984. ∞™

Contents

Preface

This guide sets forth your rights under the present law and offers suggestions on how they can be protected. It is one of a continuing series of handbooks published in cooperation with the American Civil Liberties Union (ACLU).

Surrounding these publications is the hope that Americans, informed of their rights, will be encouraged to exercise them. Through their exercise, rights are given life. If they are rarely used, they may be forgotten and violations may become routine.

This guide offers no assurances that your rights will be respected. The laws may change, and in some of the subjects covered in these pages they change quite rapidly. An effort has been made to note those parts of the law where movement is taking place, but it is not always possible to predict accurately when the law *will* change.

Even if the laws remain the same, their interpretations by courts and administrative officials often vary. In a federal system such as ours, there is a built-in problem since state and federal law differ, not to speak of the confusion between states. In addition, there are wide variations in the ways in which particular courts and administrative officials will interpret the same law at any given moment.

If you encounter what you consider to be a specific abuse of your rights, you should seek legal assistance. There are a number of agencies that may help you, among them ACLU affiliate offices, but bear in mind that the ACLU is a limited-purpose organization. In many communities, there are federally funded legal service offices which provide assistance to persons who cannot afford the costs of legal representation. In general, the rights that the ACLU defends are freedom of inquiry and expression; due process of law; equal protection of the laws; and privacy. The authors in this series have discussed other rights (even though they sometimes fall outside the ACLU's usual concern) in order to provide as much guidance as possible.

These books have been planned as guides for the people directly affected: thus the question and answer format. (In some areas there are more detailed works available for experts.) These guides seek to raise the major issues and inform the nonspecialist of the basic law on the subject. The authors of these books are themselves specialists who understand the need for information at "street level."

If you encounter a specific legal problem in an area discussed in one of these handbooks, show the book to your attorney. Of course, he or she will not be able to rely exclusively on the handbook to provide you with adequate representation. But if your attorney hasn't had a great deal of experience in the specific area, the handbook can provide helpful suggestions on how to proceed.

> Norman Dorsen, President
> American Civil Liberties Union

The principal purpose of this handbook, as well as others in this series, is to inform individuals of their legal rights. The authors from time to time suggest what the law should be, but their personal views are not necessarily those of the ACLU. For the ACLU's position on the issues discussed in this handbook the reader should write to Librarian, ACLU, 132 West 43 Street, New York, NY 10036.

Acknowledgments

The authors would like to express our appreciation to the following staff members of the National Prison Project, American Civil Liberties Union Foundation, Inc., who participated in the writing and production of this book: Elizabeth Alexander, Adjoa Aiyetoro, Alexa Freeman, Jere Krakoff, Daniel Manville, Mark Lopez, and Sharon R. Goretsky.

Introduction

As an institution, our penal and "correctional" system is an abject failure. The conditions in America's jails and prisons virtually ensure psychological impairment and physical deterioration for thousands of men and women each year.[1] Reformation and rehabilitation is the rhetoric; systematic dehumanization is the reality. Public attention is directed only sporadically toward the subhuman conditions that prevail in these institutions, and usually only because the prisoners themselves have risked many more years in confinement, and in some cases even their lives, to dramatize their situation by protest. The uprisings in Attica and New Mexico were but two examples of an undercurrent of tension, hatred, and hostility that threatens to rip apart the uneasy rule by fear which prevails in most penal institutions today.

In assessing the development of prisoners' rights law, one must keep in mind that it has been accompanied by the most massive prison population explosion ever experienced in the United States. On 30 June 1986, our sentenced prison population was 528,945, more than double what it was ten years earlier. The current rate of increase of over 10 percent per annum represents a prison space demand of about one thousand new beds a week, far in excess of new beds being supplied. Thus, in looking at the impact of litigation on conditions of confinement, we might ask: In light of this enormous population increase, what might prison conditions be today without the litigation of the last decade? The answer would be something out of Dante's *Inferno*.

Have there always been prisons?

No. It was not until the nineteenth century that the use of prisons became widespread. Until the middle of the eighteenth century, European penology was motivated principally by punishment and retribution. Most crimes were dealt with by corporal punishment and a great many by execution. Imprisonment was thought to be a deterrent to criminal activity (an idea prevalent today, although still not established through objective criteria) and was considered more humane than corporal punishment. Moreover, prisons were also built with the idea of reformation: the penitentiary was intended to serve as a place for reflection in solitude leading to repentance and redemption. But these prisons served in reality only to punish—physically and mentally. Supported by court-adopted theories that prisoners were in fact slaves of the state, prison administrators had absolutely free reign to abuse their inmates as they wished. There was no question of prisoners' "rights."

How do prisons in the United States today compare with those in other countries?

It is difficult to generalize about comparable prison conditions. Our prisons are probably better than facilities of some countries but are certainly worse than those of countries in Western Europe with very enlightened criminal justice and penal policies such as the Netherlands and the Scandinavian countries. One thing is certain, however: prison conditions in the United States suffer in great part because of the horrendous overcrowding that has developed in the past decade and which appears to be continuing. This is a direct result of our excessive reliance on the use of imprisonment as a sanction as compared to most other countries. With very little correlation to crime rates, the United States incarcerates more persons per capita than any country in the world with the exception of Russia and South Africa, and we send people to prison for far longer periods of time.[2]

Didn't the courts rule on prison conditions?

No. The courts concurred with the notion that incarceration in prison was for punishment and adopted a "hands-off" policy which prevented prisoners from securing any rights except those their jailers allowed. Few persons, including lawyers, attempted to challenge this policy. This abdication of judicial responsibility reinforced the status quo of prison life and, because no other political or social institutions responded to the prisoners' complaints, the penal system became isolated from public scrutiny.

The practical effect of the "hands-off" policy was to place all decisions concerning internal affairs of the prison within the discretion of the prison officials, no matter how arbitrary and inhumane the results. The courts continually deferred to the so-called expertise of the prison administration in refusing even to hear complaints by prisoners concerning violations of their most fundamental rights.

Do courts today rule on prison conditions?

Yes. The "hands-off" policy is now slowly being replaced by a judicial attitude that seeks to eliminate the major abuses suffered by prisoners. But despite substantial legal victories over the past fifteen years, the prisoners' lot has improved, practically speaking, only with respect to major abuses and severe physical punishment. The erosion of the "hands-off" doctrine has hardly resulted in judicial activism. Even liberal courts have failed to confront what one commentator has correctly termed the "central evil" of prison life—"the unreviewed administrative discretion granted to the poorly trained personnel who deal directly with prisoners."[3] Moreover, even those rights which are now guaranteed by the courts are often illusory for many prisoners. Implementation and enforcement of these rights rest primarily in the hands of prison officials who continue to struggle to maintain the status quo. Litigation is costly and time-consuming, and few lawyers have volunteered their service in this area. Thus, even those minimal rights which appear on paper are often in reality denied.

On what principles do courts rely in deciding prisoner rights cases?

Generally, courts rely on three principles. First, that lawful incarceration necessarily deprives a prisoner of certain rights and privileges he would enjoy in the free society; second, that a convict does not lose all of his civil rights—certain fundamental rights follow him (with appropriate limitations) through the prison gates, and are to be protected by the courts; finally, that prison officials are vested with wide discretion and unless constitutional or other fundamental rights are involved, the federal courts are reluctant to interfere with internal operations of prison discipline.[4]

This formulation of the federal courts' role in protecting prisoners' rights is sufficiently broad and contradictory that, given virtually any set of facts, a court could deny or give relief relying on one or more of the principles stated. In some cases more specific rules have been announced by the courts, but we are still far from a concise and predictable rule of law in prisons. In one of the most perceptive and enlightened opinions discussing the general constitutional framework in which prisoners' rights suits should be decided, a federal district court reasoned:

> In my view, in passing upon . . . challenges to the rules for institutional survival [censorship, body searches, summary procedures in disciplinary hearings, etc.], the balance must be struck in favor of the individual rights of the prisoners. That is to say, if one of these rules of institutional survival affects significantly a liberty which is clearly protected among the general population, and if its only justification is that the prison cannot survive without it, then it may well be that the Constitution requires that the prison be modified. Specifically, if the functions of deterrence and rehabilitation cannot be performed in a prison without the imposition of a restrictive regime not reasonably related to those functions, it may well be that those functions can no longer be performed constitutionally in a prison setting. Also, with respect to the comparatively few offenders who simply must be physically restrained for periods of time to prevent them from committing antisocial acts, it may well be that the society will be compelled, constitutionally, to allocate sufficient resources for physical facilities and manpower to permit this function of physical restraint to be performed in a setting which little resembles today's prisons.[5]

Although the Supreme Court has not departed significantly from the lower court on general conditions issues (as distinguished from First Amendment or visitation issues where they have rendered terrible decisions), they have continuously sent a disturbing message to the lower federal courts: that these courts should pay enormous deference to prison administrators and should not intervene unless there is overwhelming evidence of gross constitutional violations. Chief Justice Rehnquist put it succinctly a few years ago in a case where prisoners suffered under overcrowded conditions, stating, "Nobody promised them a rose garden."[6]

Why have courts consistently refused to look behind the

decisions of prison administrators and merely deferred to their "expertise"?

It is the answer to this question that provides an important key to understanding prison life. Judges have known for years that many prison rules and procedures are irrational, inhumane, and illegal, but they have used the "hands-off" doctrine, in effect, to avoid discussion of these problems. The obvious result is that prison officials are left with total control over the prisoners in their institutions. Of course, the more unchecked, the more arbitrary; and the more capricious the power of a prison administrator, the easier it is for him to rule. The political judgment that a "hands-off" policy indicates is, quite simply, that prisoners may be abused in whatever way their keepers desire, for this will ensure order and control in a system that is virtually bankrupt of any positive values or norms.

Who runs the prison system?

The prison system in America is an extremely diverse collection of facilities, techniques, and programs. The hundreds of thousands of commitments each year are dispersed to town, city, county, state, and federal institutions and range from the overnight lockup for the drunk or disorderly to maximum-security prisons for the long-term inmate. Each level of government operates independently of the others in administering its prisons and correctional apparatus. Thus, the federal government operates the Federal Bureau of Prisons but has no control over state corrections; each state has responsibility for its prison system but usually no control over county or city jails; and the rules and regulations vary substantially from penal institution to penal institution.

What law applies to prisons?

The only source of law applicable to all prisons is the Constitution, which provides only a minimum standard for prisoners' rights.

Ideally, state and federal statutes and administrative rules and regulations could expand these rights, but except in a few instances the Constitution continues to provide the most meaningful basis for assertion of prisoners' rights. Most state statutes vest almost complete power and discretion for rule making in prisons to an administrative board of corrections or similar board. The regulations established by these agencies rarely guarantee any significant rights for prisoners and most often only generally provide rules for the maintenance of security in the prison. For these reasons, most of the rights now guaranteed to prisoners are a result of judicial rulings rather than legislative or administrative action.

This does not mean, however, that in the assertion of prisoners' rights the statutes and rules of the prisons should be ignored. Indeed, unless prison administrators begin to change their attitudes and policies, no number of constitutional decisions will cause a perceptible change. These "paper rights" must be upheld and enforced, and that duty and power remains in the hands of prison officials.

The discussion of substantive rights that follows in the next several chapters applies fairly generally to all prisoners in the United States, but while some of these rights are now secure for all prisoners, many others are provided only in some states or federal circuits and not in others. Wherever possible, the breakdown among different jurisdictions is indicated.

Are there many court decisions in the area of prisoners' rights?

Until the late 1960s, there had been practically no court decisions dealing with the rights of prisoners. That has changed substantially during the past fifteen years. However, compared to most legal areas, the number of decisions involving prisoners' rights is small, reflecting not only the very recent change in the attitude of the courts concerning their responsibility to ensure the constitutional rights of prisoners, but also the harsh reality that only a few prisoners have the resources and courage to challenge the actions of their jailers in the courts.

The relatively small number of cases discussed, while representative of the types of complaints that prisoners have, does not accurately represent the number of prisoners who are daily denied their constitutional rights. As the knowledge of rights grows among prisoners, the court dockets show a marked increase in prisoners' rights cases. Whether the courts will meet this challenge with the Constitution remains to be seen. If they do not, however, we should not expect that prisoners will agree to continue suffering under inhumane conditions for they, too, understand the politics and dynamics of our penal system. If legal relief is not provided, other, less peaceful attempts at securing rights will surely follow, and that would be a tragedy for all concerned.

NOTES

1. *See, e.g., Pugh v. Locke,* 406 F. Supp. 318 (M.D. Ala. 1976); *Ramos v. Lamm,* 485 F. Supp. 122 (D. Colo. 1979); *Palmigiano v. Garrahy,* 443 F. Supp. 956 (D.R.I. 1977).
2. Council of Europe, *Prison Information Bulletin,* June 1985.
3. Hirschkop, "The Rights of Prisoners," in *The Rights of Americans,* at 451 (N. Dorsen, ed. 1970).
4. *See, e.g., Wolff v. McDonnell,* 418 U.S. 539, 94 S. Ct. 2963, 41 L. Ed. 2d 935 (1974); *Rhodes v. Chapman,* 452 U.S. 337, 101 S. Ct. 2392, 69 L. Ed. 2d 59 (1981).
5. *Morales v. Schmidt,* 340 F. Supp. 544 (W.D. Wis. 1972), *rev'd* 489 F.2d 1335 (7th Cir. 1973), *mod.* 494 F.2d 85 (7th Cir. 1974) *(en banc).*
6. *Atiyeh v. Capps,* 449 U.S. 1312, 101 S. Ct. 829, 66 L. Ed. 2d 785 (1981)(Rehnquist, J.)(stay granted).

THE RIGHTS OF PRISONERS

I

Freedom from Cruel and Unusual Punishment

Prisoners have an absolute right to be free from cruel and unusual punishment under the Eighth Amendment; although it is an easy matter to state the basic right, it is more difficult to specify what is included in its definition.

Historically, the Eighth Amendment's ban on cruel and unusual punishment was aimed at preventing a recurrence of torture and barbarous punishments common in England and colonial America, such as disemboweling and decapitation. During the nineteenth century, this provision was thought to be virtually obsolete as these punishments were no longer being imposed. In 1910, however, the Supreme Court gave added force to the Eighth Amendment, holding that the amendment's protections were not tied to a particular theory or point in time.[1]

Today, punishments which are not necessarily barbarous, but nonetheless involve unnecessary and unrestricted infliction of pain, are prohibited.[2] Included are those punishments that are totally without penological justification.

The Eighth Amendment rests upon fundamental considerations of human decency; it has been held to contain a "basic prohibition against inhuman treatment" and its basic underlying concept "is nothing less than the dignity of man." The amendment was designed to assure that the state's punishing power be exercised within the limits of civilized standards and it "must draw its meaning from the evolving standards of decency that mark the progress of a maturing society."[3] An 1892 Supreme Court decision provides the touchstone for the amendment's application to conditions in prisons. It held that the government is "bound to protect against lawless violence all persons in their service or custody in the course of the administration of justice."[4]

What constitutes cruel and unusual punishment?

There is presently no single "test" used to determine whether a punishment is cruel and unusual. Rather, the Supreme Court has determined the amendment flexibly. Historically, courts have considered whether: (1) the punishment shocks the general conscience of a civilized society; (2) whether the punishment is unnecessarily cruel, and (3) whether the punishment goes beyond legitimate penal aims. However, judges are not to use merely their own views as to whether a punishment is cruel and unusual, but are to base their judgment as much as possible on objective factors.[5]

With regard to conditions of confinement in prisons, the conditions must not inflict unrestricted and unnecessary pain; nor may punitive conditions greatly exceed the seriousness of the crime which brought on the imprisonment.

Obviously, in the absence of sheer barbarity or physical abuse, it is difficult to specify any one condition which might meet these definitions. However, conditions in a prison, taken together, may be so foul or inhumane as to constitute cruel and unusual punishment. It is increasingly important, then, to consider all facets of a prisoner's existence in making a claim of an Eighth Amendment violation.

Also, because courts have deferred in many cases to the judgments of prison administrators in specific areas, it is necessary to portray the entire prison experience and its effect.

What conditions in prisons amount to cruel and unusual punishment?

During the past dozen years, prison overcrowding is the one condition that has had the most serious impact on prison life. Extensive overcrowding almost never exists by itself but inevitably has an adverse impact on basic health and safety. It affects environmental health and safety, food services, medical and mental health care, and programming. It increases idleness which, together with other consequences of overcrowding, often leads to increased levels of violence.

In 1981, the Supreme Court of the United States addressed the issue of which prison conditions constitute cruel and unusual punishment for the first time.[6] The Court held that overcrowding, in this case housing two men in a cell designed for one, by itself was not unconstitutional. While the Court endorsed specific decisions of lower courts that had granted relief in prison conditions cases, it focused in this case on the lower court's failure to find specific harm to basic health and safety resulting from the overcrowding, and it rejected the lower court's reliance on generalized expert opinion. This decision makes it more difficult for prisoners to show that constitutional standards have been violated by requiring proof directly related to harm from overcrowding at the particular institution in question.

The Supreme Court in *Rhodes v. Chapman* appears to have approved of the procedure of considering conditions as a whole in prison suits. Although the Court declined to hold that the double celling of inmates is unconstitutional *per se*, the Court did state:

> Conditions other than those in *Gamble* and *Hutto,* alone or in combination, may deprive inmates of the minimal civilized measure of life's necessities. Such conditions could be cruel and unusual under the contemporary standard of decency that we recognized in *Gamble*. (452 U.S. at 347)

Several courts have held that prison conditions, taken as a whole and in some cases individually, amount to cruel and unusual punishment. For example, in a case involving the Rhode Island Adult Correctional Institutions, United States District Judge Pettine stated:

> The evidence is overwhelming that the totality of conditions of confinement in Maximum and Medium do not provide the "tolerable living environment" . . . that the Eighth and Fourteenth Amendments require for state prison inmates. . . .The lack of sanitation, lighting, heating, and ventilation, and the noise, idleness, fear and violence, and the absence or inadequacy of programs of classification, education, physical exercise, vocational training or other constructive activity create a total environment where debilitation is inevitable, and which is unfit for human habitation and shocking to the conscience of a reasonably civilized person.

The judge had found leaking and inadequate plumbing, filth, roaches and rodents, and an inadequate maintenance program. The amount of lighting was less than that necessary for safe reading. The noise level was maddening, the heating and ventilation systems were not minimally adequate, and there were numerous fire hazards. Violence and the fear of violence existed throughout the system.[7]

Despite the added difficulty of proving that conditions of confinement amount to cruel and unusual punishment since the *Rhodes* decision, a number of federal courts have continued to grant far-ranging relief in prison and jail cases where over-crowding was combined with an adverse impact on the basic health and safety of inmates.[8]

Is solitary confinement cruel and unusual punishment?

It can be. A claim of cruel and unusual punishment need not be based on the totality of prison life. It may also be established by reference to a particular condition of confine-ment. It should surprise no one that most cases raising the issue of cruel and unusual punishment concern confinement in segregation, strip-cells, or solitary. No court has ruled that confinement in segregation or solitary confinement is cruel and unusual punishment *per se*. To the contrary, numerous cases around the country have upheld the use of solitary confinement. However, the courts have drawn limits as to what kinds of physical conditions and treatment may be tolerated. One court was so appalled by conditions in isolation that it entered a corrective order immediately after trial. The court stated:

> The indescribable conditions in the isolation cells required immediate action to protect inmates from any further tor-ture by confinement in those cells. As many as six inmates were packed in four foot by eight foot cells with no beds, no lights, no running water, and a hole in the floor for a toilet which could only be flushed from the outside. The infamous Draper "doghouse" is a separate building, locked from the outside, with no guard stationed inside. Inmates in punitive isolation received only one meal per day, fre-quently without utensils. They were permitted no exercise or reading material and could shower only every 11 days.[9]

Other cases in which courts have declared conditions in solitary to be cruel and unusual include the following: In a Tennessee prison, the inmate was placed in a five foot by eight foot cell, unlighted, and made to sleep nude on the floor. There was only a hole in the floor for his wastes, and the flushing of this matter was controlled by a guard outside the cell.[10]

In Arkansas the federal courts have ruled in several cases that where solitary confinement is in dirty, overcrowded, vermin-infested cells, without proper ventilation, with limited opportunity for exercise and dirty food, the proscription against cruel and unusual punishment is violated.[11]

A New York federal court ruled that conditions in solitary confinement in state prisons were cruel and unusual where the complaining inmates were kept nude; had only a blanket on the bare floor on which to sleep; had no light, radio or smoking privileges; had to stand all day; and had only a toilet and washbowl, but no toilet paper, in the cell.[12] The court said:

> "We are of the view that civilized standards of humane decency simply do not permit a man for a substantial period of time to be denuded and exposed to the bitter cold. . . .and to be deprived of the basic elements of hygiene such as soap and toilet paper."[13]

But in Texas, a federal court upheld solitary confinement where the prison provided a wash basin, drinking fountain, steel bunk without a mattress, blanket, cloth gown, toothbrush and a shower every other day, even though the cell was kept in complete darkness and the daily diet was bread and water with a "full" meal every seventy-two hours.[14]

Are there any restrictions on the imposition of solitary confinement?

Yes. Solitary confinement may also be cruel and unusual where the reason for isolation or the length of incarceration in isolation is not justified by the alleged violation of prison regulations, even though the physical conditions do not fall below the standards required by the Eighth Amendment.

Thus, a federal district court ruled that sixteen months in disciplinary segregation for a work stoppage was disproportionate to the offense and unconstitutional.[15] Moreover, a court in Washington D.C. ruled that isolation in solitary confinement for two years constituted cruel and unusual punishment because the only violation of prison rules—engaging in a demonstration tending to breach the peace—was relatively minor.[16]

However, numerous courts have held certain periods of isolation not to constitute cruel and unusual punishment, and some have held that isolation may be indefinite.[17]

Have any specific punishments been held to be cruel and unusual?

Yes. The courts have established minimal requirements for individual aspects of confinement in solitary. For example, one court has limited the use of mechanical restraints on inmates confined to isolation.[18] Inmates in solitary also have a right to a reasonable opportunity for physical exercise. In Georgia, a federal district court has held that there was no constitutionally acceptable justification for denying segregated prisoners a chance to exercise,[19] and a federal district court in Louisiana ruled that where an inmate on death row was allowed out of his small cell for only fifteen minutes a day, in which time he was to bathe, exercise, and wash clothes, the constitutional proscription against cruel and unusual punishment was violated. The court held that confinement for long periods of time without the opportunity for regular outdoor exercise violates the Eighth Amendment.[20]

In Virginia a federal district court has enjoined the practice of providing only bread and water to prisoners. Noting that such a diet provides a daily intake of only seven hundred calories compared to the average need of two thousand calories for sedentary men, and taking judicial notice that such a diet is deficient as well with respect to other necessary dietary elements, the court concluded that the resultant pangs of hunger constitute a dull, prolonged sort of corporal punishment.[21]

One court has permitted visits to men in a segregation unit even though they had refused an order to shave.[22] The Seventh Circuit has barred the use of tranquilizing drugs to punish juveniles.[23] The court did say, however, that authorities could use the drugs in an ongoing therapeutic program.

Is corporal punishment allowed in prisons?

No. Most states by regulation forbid the imposition of corporal punishment. Additionally, the Court of Appeals for the Eighth Circuit has ruled, in enjoining the use of the strap (for whipping), that any form of corporal punishment is cruel and unusual punishment within the meaning of the Constitution.[24]

The Virginia Federal District Court also invalidated several other facets of punishment that had been used in the Virginia state prisons. First, the practice of controlling misbehavior by placing inmates in chains or handcuffs in their cells was held unjustified since the result of such punishment was, in various cases, the infliction of permanent scars, lack of sleep, and prolonged physical pain. In addition, the court prohibited officials from taking away an inmate's clothing unless a doctor states in writing that the inmate's health will not thereby be affected and that the inmate presents a substantial risk of injuring him- or herself if given garments. The use of tear gas was also enjoined. It was pointed out that prison officials had other, far less drastic means available for enforcing discipline in the prison.[25]

Are prison officials liable for the use of excessive force during prison disturbances?

Generally not. In *Whitley v. Albers*,[26] the Supreme Court ruled on a case involving a prison disturbance in which a staff member was taken hostage. The prison official in charge yelled, "Shoot the bastards," and a prisoner who had not taken part in the disturbance was shot while running away. The Supreme Court held that, based on these facts, a jury could not be allowed to find, under the Eighth Amendment or the Due Process Clause, any prison staff liable for the injuries because the actions were shown not to indicate a bad faith, wanton infliction of pain with no legitimate purpose. Errors of judgment that result in the excessive use of force do not violate the Constitution. Thus, the *Whitley* standard makes it very difficult for a plaintiff to get to a jury in virtually any use-of-force case.

Do prisoners have a right to be protected against sexual assault?

In recent years, several degrading and unconstitutional facets of prison life have become exposed to public view and scrutiny. These problems have been highlighted again and again in court cases, administrative studies, and legislative investigations. Perhaps the most dramatic and sickening aspect of these disclosures, however, concerns the widespread and often uncontrolled pattern of assaults by prisoners and guards upon prisoners.

No penal institution in the country remains free of this problem. In Philadelphia, for example, the Davis Report on Sexual Assaults in the Philadelphia prison system conservatively estimated that during a 26-month period, there were approxi-

mately 2000 sexual assaults involving approximately 1500
individual victims and 3500 individual aggressors.

The court in Alabama described the situation in the Alabama
prisons as follows:

> Inmates are housed in virtually unguarded, overcrowded
> dormitories, with no realistic attempt by officials to sep-
> arate violent, aggressive inmates from those who are pas-
> sive or weak. The tension generated by idleness and
> deplorable living conditions contributes further to the ever-
> present threat of violence from which inmates have no
> refuge.[27]

Many court decisions have recognized the rape problem.
Claims by prisoners that prison authorities have not provided
adequate protection have been upheld,[28] and in the context of
escape prosecutions, courts have sustained proof of prior sexual
assaults as a valid defense.[29] For several years now it has been
clear that under the Eighth Amendment, prisoners are entitled
to protection from the assaults of other prisoners.[30]

What remedies does a prisoner have if assaulted?

The Supreme Court has recently placed substantial limitations on the remedies available in federal court to prisoners
who are assaulted or injured in prison. In one case, the Court
ruled that a prisoner who slipped on a pillow left negligently
on the stairs by a corrections officer could not sue prison officials
in federal court for negligence even though there was no remedy available to him in state court.[31] The Supreme Court said
that the Due Process Clause of the Constitution is not implicated by a state official's negligent act because there must be
a deliberate decision by the state official to cause the injury to
the prisoner.

In another case decided the same day, the Supreme Court
extended this reasoning to quite a different set of facts.[32] In
this case, a prisoner advised prison officials that he had been
threatened by another prisoner. The officials did nothing about
the warning, and two days later the prisoner was attacked by
the other prisoner and sustained serious injuries. Because the
attorneys and the district court characterized this claim as negligence only, the Supreme Court said there was no constitutional violation alleged or proven.

A prisoner may, however, have some remedy available under the common law of a particular state, and if a prisoner suffers injuries caused by an unjustified attack by prison guards[33] or by another prisoner where officials simply stood by and permitted the attack to proceed,[34] a federal constitutional claim could be maintained. Moreover, the Supreme Court left open the possibility that claims based on recklessness or gross negligence would be sufficient "to trigger the protection of the Due Process Claims."[35]

Is sexual deprivation considered cruel and unusual?

No. The denial of conjugal visits presents an important question with respect to the prohibition against cruel and unusual punishment. Heterosexual deprivation is the rule, of course, in virtually every prison in this country. This condition causes anxiety and aggression, frustrates rehabilitation, and disrupts family relationships. Nevertheless, most people accept this enforced abstinence as a legitimate part of prison life, and it has never been held to be cruel and unusual punishment. In this area, our correctional system falls far behind those of many other countries which allow furloughs and conjugal visits.

NOTES

1. *Weems v. United States*, 217 U.S. 349, 30 S. Ct. 544, 54 L. Ed. 2d 793 (1910).
2. *Rhodes v. Chapman*, 452 U.S. 337, 101 S. Ct. 2392, 69 L. Ed. 2d 59 (1981); *Gregg v. Georgia*, 428 U.S. 153, 96 S. Ct. 2909, 49 L. Ed. 2d 859 (1976).
3. *Trop v. Dulles*, 356 U.S. 86, 100–101, 78 S. Ct. 590, 2 L. Ed. 2d 630 (1958).
4. *Logan v. United States*, 144 U.S. 263, 12 S. Ct. 617, 36 L. Ed. 2d 429 (1892).
5. *Rhodes v. Chapman, supra* note 2.
6. *Id.*
7. *Palmigiano v. Garrahy*, 443 F. Supp. 956 (D.R.I. 1977).
8. *See* for example, *Toussaint v. Yockey*, 722 F.2d 1490 (9th Cir. 1984); *Ruiz v. Estelle*, 679 F.2d 1115, *modified* 688 F.2d 266 (5th Cir. 1982), *cert. denied*, 103 S. Ct. 1438 (1983); *Wellman v. Faulkner*, 715 F.2d 269 (7th Cir. 1983), *cert. denied*, 104 S. Ct. 3587 (1984); *French v.*

Owens, 538 F. Supp. 910 (S.D. Ind. 1982), *aff'd in pertinent part,* 777 F.2d 1250 (7th Cir. 1985); *Martino v. Carey,* 563 F. Supp. 984 (D. Or. 1983); *Fischer v. Winter,* 564 F. Supp. 281 (N.D. Cal. 1983); *Cody v. Hillard,* 599 F. Supp. 1025 (D.S.D. 1984); *Monmouth County Correctional Inst. Inmates v. Lanzano,* 595 F. Supp. 1417 (D.N.J. 1984); *Grubbs v. Bradley,* 552 F. Supp. 1052 (M.D. Tenn. 1982); *Vazquez v. Gray,* 523 F. Supp. 1359 (S.D.N.Y. 1981), and *Ramos v. Lamm,* 520 F. Supp. 1059 (D. Colo. 1981), *on remand from* 639 F.2d 559 (10th Cir. 1980).

9. *Pugh v. Locke,* 406 F. Supp. 318 (M.D. Ala. 1976), *aff'd and remanded sub nom. Newman v. Alabama,* 559 F.2d 283 (5th Cir. 1977), *rev'd in part on other grounds sub nom. Alabama v. Pugh,* 438 U.S. 781, 98 S. Ct. 3057, 56 L. Ed. 2d 1114 (1978).

10. *Hancock v. Avery,* 301 F. Supp. 786 (M.D. Tenn. 1969).

11. *Holt v. Sarver,* 309 F. Supp. 362 (E.D. Ark. 1970).

12. *Wright v. McMann,* 387 F.2d 519 (2d Cir. 1967).

13. *Id.* at 526. *See also LaReau v. MacDougall,* 473 F.2d 974 (2d Cir. 1972); *Finney v. Arkansas Bd. of Corrections,* 505 F.2d 194 (8th Cir. 1974); *Berch v. Stahl,* 373 F. Supp. 412 (W.D.N.C. 1974).

14. *Novak v. Beto,* 453 F.2d 661 (5th Cir. 1971). *See also Gregory v. Wyse,* 512 F.2d 378 (10th Cir. 1975) and *Benfield v. Bounds,* 363 F. Supp. 160 (E.D.N.C. 1973).

15. *Adams v. Carlson,* 368 F. Supp. 1050 (E.D. Ill. 1973). *See also Hardwick v. Ault,* 447 F. Supp. 116 (M.D. Ga. 1978).

16. *Fulwood v. Clemmer,* 206 F. Supp. 370 (D.D.C. 1962).

17. *La Plante v. Southworth,* 484 F. Supp. 115 (D.R.I. 1980)(120 days not excessive); *Nelson v. Collins,* 455 F. Supp. 727 (D. Md. 1978).

18. *Stewart v. Rhodes,* 473 F. Supp. 1185 (S.D. Ohio 1979).

19. *Krist v. Smith,* 309 F. Supp. 497 (S.D. Ga. 1970). *See also Harris v. Bell,* 402 F. Supp. 469 (W.D. Mo. 1975)(one-hour daily outdoor exercise ordered for juveniles in segregation).

20. *Sinclair v. Henderson,* 331 F. Supp. 1123 (E.D. La. 1971).

21. *Landman v. Royster,* 333 F. Supp. 621 (E.D. Va. 1971).

22. *Agron v. Montanye,* 392 F. Supp. 454 (W.D.N.Y. 1975).

23. *Nelson v. Heyne,* 491 F.2d 352 (7th Cir. 1974).

24. *Jackson v. Bishop,* 404 F.2d 571 (8th Cir. 1968).

25. *Landman v. Royster, supra. See also Knecht v. Gillman,* 488 F.2d 1136 (8th Cir. 1973)(forced drugs improperly used as a method of punishment for minor offenses). *But see Spain v. Procunier,* 600 F.2d 189 (9th Cir. 1979)(some use of tear gas *may* be justified).

26. __U.S.__, 106 S. Ct. 1078, 89 L. Ed. 2d 251 (1986).

27. *Pugh v. Locke, supra* note 9, at 324.

28. *Van Horn v. Lukhard,* 392 F. Supp. 384 (E.D. Va. 1975) and *Carroll v. Jones,* 17 Crim. L. Rptr. 2240 (4th Cir. 1975).
29. *People v. Harmon,* 395 Mich. 625, 232 N.W.2d 187 (1975) and *People v. Lovercamp,* 118 Cal. 110 (1974).
30. *Little v. Walker,* 552 F.2d 193 (7th Cir. 1977). *Also see Withers v. Levine,* 615 F.2d 158 (4th Cir. 1980).
31. *Daniels v. Williams,* __U.S.__, 106 S. Ct. 662, 88 L. Ed. 2d 662 (1986).
32. *Davidson v. Cannon,* __U.S.__, 106 S. Ct. 668, 88 L. Ed. 2d 667 (1986).
33. *Johnson v. Glick,* 481 F.2d 1028 (2d Cir. 1973), *cert. denied* 414 U.S. 1033 (1973).
34. *Curtis v. Everette,* 489 F.2d 516 (3d Cir. 1973), *cert. denied* 416 U.S. 995 (1974).
35. *Daniels v. Williams, supra,* note 31 at 667, n.3.

II
Due Process

When a person is lawfully imprisoned by the state, he loses many of the freedoms, rights, and privileges that ordinary citizens take for granted. This is the nature of incarceration and the substance of punishment. But the courts have consistently held that even while in prison persons retain certain liberty interests which cannot be deprived without the protections of constitutional due process. Here we discuss the extent and limitations of due process as required by the courts, particularly in regard to disciplinary hearings, institutional transfers, and protection of personal property.

Do prisoners have a right to due process at prison disciplinary proceedings?

Historically, prisoners were given few, if any, of the rights normally guaranteed by the Due Process Clause. Before the courts started to intervene, prison administrators had total power to make rules, usually vague and unwritten; enforce them, usually inconsistently; and arbitrarily prescribe punishment. That prisoners' due process rights at disciplinary proceedings have now been addressed by the courts is important because disciplinary proceedings affect a large number of prisoners and can result in serious consequences. Findings of misconduct can lead to revocation of prison privileges (visits, access to reading material, recreation), placement in segregation, involuntary transfer to another penal institution, and denial of parole.

The Supreme Court of the United States has in recent years addressed a number of these issues. The details of its decisions will be discussed later in this chapter.

How are disciplinary matters dealt with in the prison context?

Disciplinary proceedings are usually initiated upon a complaint of a guard or other prison official that a prisoner has violated a prison rule or regulation. The matter is then referred to the prison disciplinary committee ("adjustment committee," "prison board") for disposition. This committee is usually composed of prison officials such as the warden, associate warden, or classification officers.

From here, the process differs from state to state and institution to institution. Usually, the procedure followed is to conduct a hearing at which the committee or disciplinary board meets with the prisoner, notifies him of the charges, and allows him an opportunity to respond.

What are the possible results of a disciplinary proceeding?

Various forms of dispositions and punishment can be ordered as a result of these hearings. In some cases the charge will be dismissed, and no change in status will occur. Available statistics indicate, however, that in most cases some form of punishment is ordered. For institutional offenses, the punishment may take the form of revocation of prison privileges for a certain period of time, short-term placement in segregation, involuntary transfer to another penal institution (usually one that has a higher form of security), loss of accumulated good time, and—most ominously—referral of the disciplinary finding to the parole board for its consideration upon an inmate's application for release on parole.

Which due process rights are prisoners entitled to at disciplinary hearings?

The Supreme Court of the United States has issued opinions in a number of cases that spell out the kind of due process rights that prisoners are entitled to at disciplinary hearings. The first case in which the Supreme Court addressed this issue was *Wolff v. McDonnell.*[1] The Court said that although a prisoner's rights are diminished by virtue of incarceration, "there is no iron curtain drawn between the Constitution and the prisons of this country." The Court ruled that before a prisoner could be seriously penalized for a disciplinary violation (the serious penalties in this case being the taking away of good time credits and/or solitary confinement), the state must provide certain minimum procedures. A prisoner is entitled to at least 24-hour written notice of the charges against him, the right to call witnesses and present documentary evidence in his defense (when doing so would not be unduly hazardous to institutional safety or correctional goals), the right to an impartial hearing body, and the right to a written statement by the hearing body about the evidence it relied on and the reasons for whatever disciplinary action it takes.

The Court declined to grant the right to cross-examination of witnesses. Further, the Court ruled that there was no right to counsel at proceedings even if the incident might lead to criminal charges.[2] Of course, prison officials may permit confrontation of witnesses and representation by counsel or counsel-substitute.

While due process requires an impartial tribunal, courts will not find a lack of impartiality just because the committee contains security personnel. To show a lack of impartiality, something more specific must be proven. For example, a tribunal is not impartial if a committee member was involved in the incident as a participant or as a witness.[3]

There is a right to a hearing within a reasonable period of time (usually specified in the prison regulations), although given different circumstances, the courts have allowed delays ranging from seven days to two months.[4] A prisoner may be placed in administrative segregation pending the investigation and hearing of a misconduct charge, but such action must be based on some security need and cannot be used to unfairly punish a prisoner.[5]

Prison officials' use of confidential informants without disclosing their identity or, sometimes, even the details of their testimony may be permitted. The courts have held that such statements may be used without identifying the informant and without his appearance before the disciplinary committee.[6] However, in *Helms v. Hewitt*,[7] the Court of Appeals condemned reliance on hearsay statements by confidential informants without any guarantees of reliability because it "invites disciplinary sanctions on the basis of trumped up charges."

In *Ponte v. Real*,[8] prison officials had given no reasons at the hearing as to why the prisoner was not allowed to call certain witnesses in his defense. The Court ruled that the reasons must be provided at some point but that the officials have the choice of stating these reasons at the disciplinary hearing or in response to a court suit challenging the denial of witnesses. And the reason for the refusal to call witnesses must be "logically related to preventing undue hazards to institutional safety or correctional goals."[9]

In further regard to a prisoner's defense, refusal to permit a prisoner access to records that would support his defense may be unconstitutional.[10] A prisoner may refuse to testify or offer an explanation of his version of the events (in an attempt to protect the Fifth Amendment right against self-incrimination with respect to any possible criminal charges) although his silence may be considered as evidence in the disciplinary proceeding.[11] But a prisoner's silence is not sufficient evidence, by itself, to prove misconduct.

Superintendent v. Hill,[12] held that a decision revoking good-time credits must be supported by some evidence of the inmate's wrongful conduct, thus providing some minimal protection against arbitrary rulings in these hearings. Therefore, prison officials must show some affirmative evidence of wrongdoing.[13]

Of course, as discussed in other sections of this book (see chapters 9 and 11), some state courts have provided broader and fairer protections under state law or state constitutions.[14] Prisoners should always consider the state courts as a possibly more receptive forum for their complaints.

Who decides what conduct is illegal?

The prison guards. The present system puts absolute discretion and day-to-day power over every aspect of a prisoner's life in their hands. It is this part of prison life which causes the deepest resentment among prisoners, for, to a large extent, the manner in which an inmate is treated by the guards determines the severity of conditions he will have to endure. It is a regrettable fact that the lower the level of authority in prison (from warden down to guard), the greater the discretion that is vested in the prison official and the less willing the courts are to review their decisions. Thus, whether it be a request for medical treatment or the right to go to the yard or prison library or the potentially more serious matter of discipline and punishment, the guard on the block holds ultimate power over the prisoner. Complete discretion in the context of prison life where no remedies exist to correct it, can be catastrophic. Judge Sobeloff put it bluntly:

> In fact, prison guards may be more vulnerable to the corrupting influence of unchecked authority than most people. It is well known that prisons are operated on minimum budgets and that poor salaries and working conditions make it difficult to attract high-calibre personnel.

Moreover, the "training" of the officers in dealing with obstreperous prisoners is but a euphemism in most states.[15]

An inmate at Holmesburg Prison in Philadelphia understated the problem when he testified that physical brutality was not the major problem in prison. It was instead "that the guard doesn't realize how important his authority is" and that the resentment among prisoners is most clearly traceable to the guards manifesting an attitude in which the prisoner is regarded as "something less than an human being."

What kinds of punishment require due process protection?
In *Wolff*, the Supreme Court required procedural due process protection for inmates when punishment involved solitary confinement or the loss of statutory good time. But the Court has not required procedural protections for prisoners placed in administrative segregation.[16] "Keeplock," or confinement in a prisoner's own cell with loss of privileges, was found by a federal appeals court to be within the category of punishments covered by *Wolff's* protections.[17] Other kinds of punishments which have been allowed without procedural due process include loss of movie or commissary privileges,[18] three-days' cell restriction,[19] and loss of visiting privileges.[20]

The decisions in these types of cases have been inconsistent among the federal circuits because the courts have used differing theories to analyze the cases. In some instances, courts have invoked the "grievous loss" or "substantial deprivation" theory to determine whether any protective procedures were required. In those cases, the court examined the actual substance of the punishment, then weighed the severity of the punishment against those described in *Wolff*. If the court determined that the punishment inflicted in the case before it was as severe as the punishments at issue in *Wolff*, procedural due process would be required.

Courts have also utilized the "state-created right" or "liberty interest" theory which derives from *Meachum v. Fano*.[21] In these cases, the court determines whether the prisoner is being deprived of an interest or right which has been granted to him pursuant to a rule, statute, or regulation promulgated by the state. If no such interest can be found by the court, then the deprivation of such interest will not require procedural due process. This test tends to be more restrictive and allows greater discretion to prison administrators in controlling prisoner populations. The Supreme Court is clearly allowing broader discretion for prison officials, in spite of the attendant loss of rights to procedural due process for prisoners.

Are prisoners entitled to any due process safeguards when they are being classified or before they are transferred from one prison to another?

As a general rule, prison officials have absolute discretion to classify and transfer prisoners from one institution to another, even where the transfer is to a more secure and restrictive institution.[22] The Supreme Court has ruled that a conviction extinguishes any liberty interests with respect to location of imprisonment. There are two important exceptions to this rule: (1) where the transfer is made to punish a prisoner for engaging in constitutionally protected activity,[23] or (2) where a state law or prison regulation itself limits the officials' discretion by requiring a hearing or by conditioning a transfer on certain specific facts or circumstances.[24]

The harshness of the general rule allowing any classification or transfer can be seen in the case of *Olim v. Wakinekona*.[25] A Hawaii state prisoner was transferred four thousand miles to a California prison because he was considered a "troublemaker." As state law gave a prison administrator total discretion on transfer matters, the Supreme Court found no limitations that would create any liberty interest held by the prisoner. The fact that this type of transfer would effectively sever all ties that he had with family, friends, and counsel was insufficient to create any liberty interest that would require a fair hearing.

By contrast, in *Hewitt v. Helms*,[26] the Court ruled that where state law limited the officials' power to place an inmate in administrative segregation, a due process hearing was required. In that case, state regulations provided for some procedural protections and restricted the use of administrative segregation to certain specified circumstances. Other courts have similarly ruled that state law restrictions or limitations on an official's power to classify or transfer mandates a due process hearing.[27]

Where a hearing is required with respect to transfer to administrative segregation or another facility, it may not be necessary to provide due process protections to the same extent as is mandated where serious disciplinary sanctions are imposed. *In Hewitt v. Helms,* the Court stated that:

> an informal nonadversary role is sufficient both for the decision that an inmate represents a security threat and the decision to confine an inmate to administrative segregation pending completion of an investigation into misconduct charges against him. An inmate must merely receive some notice of the charges against him and an opportunity to present his views to the prison official charged with deciding whether to transfer him to administrative segregation. Ordinarily a written statement by the inmate will accomplish this purpose, although prison administrators may find it more useful to permit oral presentations in cases where they believe a written statement would be ineffective.[28]

As mentioned, transfers made in retaliation for the exercise of constitutionally protected rights, such as filing lawsuits against prisons, are in violation of a prisoner's rights. Similarly, transfers that substantially interfere with access to the courts or to counsel (for pretrial inmates) are also unlawful.[29]

Liberty interests protected by the Fourteenth Amendment are also implicated when a prisoner is transferred to a mental institution. The Supreme Court in 1980 held unconstitutional a Nebraska statute which allowed the transfer of prisoners to mental hospitals.[30] Because "[t]he loss of liberty produced by an involuntary commitment is more than a loss of freedom from confinement," such transfers require the protections of procedural due process, including notice and a hearing at which the prisoner is provided qualified and independent assistance.

How can arbitrary treatment of inmates by prison authorities be curbed?

The only way that we will ever have prisons that operate with a substantial degree of justice and fairness is when all concerned—staff and prisoners alike—share in a meaningful way the decision-making process and share the making of rules and their enforcement. This should not mean an "inmate advisory committee" in name only. Nor is the only alternative necessarily a prisoner union. Even though that may be a legitimate concept, it is one that apparently enrages most prison administrators, and the Supreme Court has permitted prison officials to bar any union activity. However, if we are to instill in people a respect for the democratic process, which is how the free world attempts to live, we are not achieving that by forcing people to live in the most totalitarian institution that we have in our society. Thus, ways must be developed to involve prisoners in the process of making decisions that affect every aspect of their life in prison.

What remedies are available when officials take or destroy a prisoner's personal property?
In *Parratt v. Taylor*,[31] prison officials had negligently lost a hobby kit that had been mailed to a prisoner. When the prisoner sued for damages, the Court ruled that where the state provided its own remedy, there was no deprivation of property without due process of law. The due process was provided by the state system of redress.

The issue was extended in *Hudson v. Palmer*[32] to intentional deprivations of property. In *Hudson,* prison guards had deliberately destroyed an inmate's property during a search of his cell. Because the state provided a remedy for such actions, the Supreme Court ruled that there were no due process violations and that no federal suit could be maintained.

Therefore, if a prisoner's property is lost, misplaced, or destroyed, the prisoner must make use of any available state administrative or court process. In some states there are simplified grievance mechanisms that will compensate the prisoner; in others, a lawsuit may be required. Only if no remedy is available in the state system may the prisoner claim a due proccess violation in federal court.

Of course, if the destruction of property was done in retaliation for the exercise of constitutional rights, a claim can be made in federal court.[33] For example, if the action was taken because the prisoner had filed a complaint or won a lawsuit against prison officials, there is a violation of the right to free access to the courts under the First and Fourteenth Amendments. In those circumstances, even if there is a state remedy the prisoner may choose to file a state or federal lawsuit. And if religious materials are seized, a First Amendment claim can be made directly in federal court.

NOTES

1. 418 U.S. 539, 94 S. Ct. 2963, 41 L. Ed. 2d 935 (1974).

2. *Baxter v. Palmigiano*, 425 U.S. 308, 96 S. Ct. 1551, 47 L. Ed. 2d 810 (1976).

3. *Powell v. Ward*, 487 F. Supp. 917 (S.D.N.Y. 1980), *aff'd as modified*, 643 F.2d 924 (2d Cir. 1981).

4. *See, e.g., Powell v. Ward, supra; Pitts v. Keve*, 511 F. Supp. 497 (D.Del. 1981); *U.S. ex rel. Houston v. Warden*, 635 F.2d 656 (7th Cir. 1980).

5. *See Hughes v. Rowe*, 449 U.S. 5, 101 S. Ct. 173, 66 L. Ed. 2d 163 (1980); *Hewitt v. Helms*, 459 U.S. 460, 477, n.9, 103 S. Ct. 864, 74 L. Ed. 2d 675 (1983); *Hendrix v. Faulkner*, 525 F. Supp. 435 (N.D.Ind. 1981).

6. *Kyle v. Hanberry*, 677 F.2d 1386 (11th Cir. 1982); *McCollum v. Miller*, 695 F.2d 1044 (7th Cir. 1982).

7. 655 F.2d 487 (3d Cir. 1981), *rev'd on other grounds, sub nom. Hewitt v. Helms*, 459 U.S. 460 (1983).

8. 471 U.S. 491, 105 S. Ct. 2192, 86 L. Ed. 2d 356 (1985).

9. *Ponte v. Real, supra*, 105 S. Ct. at 2196.

10. *Chavis v. Rowe*, 643 F.2d 1281 (7th Cir. 1981); *Pace v. Oliver*, 634 F.2d 302 (5th Cir. 1981).

11. *Baxter v. Palmigiano, supra* note 2.

12. 472 U.S. 445, 105 S. Ct. 2768, 86 L. Ed. 2d 356 (1985).

13. *Baxter v. Palmigiano, supra* note 2.

14. *McGinnes v. Stevens*, 543 P.2d 1221 (Alaska 1975) (more protections than granted by *Wolff*).

15. *Landman v. Peyton*, 370 F.2d 135, 140 (4th Cir. 1966).

16. *Hewitt v. Helms, supra* note 5.

17. *McKinnon v. Patterson*, 568 F.2d 930 (2d Cir. 1977).

18. *Gibson v. McEvers*, 631 F.2d 95 (7th Cir. 1980).

19. *Jordan v. Jones*, 625 F.2d 750 (6th Cir. 1980).

20. *Jones v. Diamond*, 594 F.2d 997 (5th Cir. 1979).

21. 427 U.S. 215, 96 S. Ct. 2532, 49 L. Ed. 2d 451 (1976).

22. *Id.*

23. *Montanye v. Haymes*, 427 U.S. 236, 96 S. Ct. 2543, 49 L. Ed. 2d 466 (1976), *on remand, Haymes v. Montanye*, 547 F.2d 188 (2d Cir. 1976).

24. *Hewitt v. Helms, supra* note 5.

25. 461 U.S. 238, 103 S. Ct. 1741, 75 L. Ed. 2d 813 (1983).

26. *Supra* note 5.

27. *E.g., Drayton v. Robinson*, 719 F.2d 1214 (3d Cir. 1983); *Bills v. Henderson*, 631 F.2d 1287 (6th Cir. 1980); *Stringer v. Rowe*, 616 F.2d 993 (7th Cir. 1980).

28. 459 U.S. at 476.
29. *Cobb v. Aytch,* 643 F.2d 946 (3d Cir. 1981)(*en banc*).
30. *Vitek v. Jones,* 445 U.S. 480, 100 S. Ct. 1254, 63 L. Ed. 2d 552 (1980).
31. 451 U.S. 527, 101 S. Ct. 1908, 68 L. Ed. 2d 420 (1981).
32. 468 U.S. 517, 104 S. Ct. 3194, 82 L. Ed. 2d 391 (1984).
33. *Montanye v. Haymes, supra* note 23.

III

Free Communication and Access
to the Courts:
The Problems of Prison Censorship

Do prisoners have the right to freedom of communication?
The United States Supreme Court has made it clear that
prisoners retain certain First Amendment rights. As Justice
Marshall stated in a concurring opinion in a leading case, *Procunier v. Martinez*:

> When the prison gates slam behind an inmate, he does
> not lose his human quality; his mind does not become
> closed to ideas; his intellect does not cease to feed on a
> free and open interchange of opinions; his yearning for
> self-respect does not end; nor is his quest for self-reali-
> zation concluded. If anything, the needs for identity and
> self-respect are more compelling in the dehumanizing
> prison environment. Whether an O. Henry writing his
> short stories in a jail cell or a frightened young inmate
> writing his family, a prisoner needs a medium for self-
> expression.[1]

In the same case, the Court established a two-part test for
determining whether prison censorship policies are valid:

> First, the regulation or practice in question must further
> an important or substantial government interest unrelated
> to the suppression of expression. . . .Security, order and
> rehabilitation. . . .Second, the limitation of First Amend-
> ment freedoms must be no greater than necessary or es-
> sential to the protection of the governmental interest
> involved. Thus a restriction on inmate correspondence that
> furthers an important or substantial interest of penal
> administration will nevertheless be invalid if its sweep is
> unnecessarily broad.[2]

Recent decisions have tended to restrict censorship practices
and, in conjunction with liberalized administrative rules and

policies, have established for many prisoners a right to freer communications with attorneys, the courts, and government officials. However, limitations on correspondence and reading materials are still prevalent, primarily because the courts continue to give undue deference to prison officials' claims for the need for censorship. Most recently, the Supreme Court has upheld inmate-to-inmate mail restrictions, but at the same time the Court reaffirmed the validity of the *Martinez* test when the challenge is to prisoner correspondence with "members of the general public."[3]

Do prisoners have the right to correspond with their lawyers, the courts, and government officials?

Yes. The greatest degree of protection thus far afforded to prisoners' correspondence has been with the courts, counsel, and government officials. In a relatively early decision, the United States Supreme Court in *Ex Parte Hull*[4] struck down a prison regulation providing that all legal documents, prior to being forwarded to a court, were subject to a prison official's determination as to whether they were properly drawn. This regulation was held to be an abridgment on the right to petition a federal court for a writ of habeas corpus. In so holding, the court indicated that the question of whether a writ was proper in form or substance was for the courts to determine; it was not a matter for a decision by a prison official.

While it is clear that an institution may not refuse to mail court-, attorney-, and government-directed letters, whether and under what circumstances prison officials may open and read them is not as clear.

The courts have provided different rules for incoming and outgoing mail. Several courts have ruled that the prison may not open, read, or in any other way interfere with official outgoing mail.[5] Moreover, because this mail often is a prisoner's only access to a court, the Supreme Court has required prisons to facilitate this process. In *Bounds v. Smith*, the Court stated:

> It is indisputable that indigent inmates must be provided at state expense with paper and pen to draft legal documents with notarial services to authenticate them, and with stamps to mail them. States must forego collection

of docket fees otherwise payable to the treasury and expend funds for transcripts.[6]

The rule for incoming official mail is more restrictive. In *Wolff v. McDonnell*, the Supreme Court considered whether letters from attorneys may be opened by prison officials in the presence of the prisoner, or whether such mail must be delivered unopened as long as there is no evidence of contraband. The Court concluded: "[W]e think that [the prison officials], by acceding to a rule whereby the inmate is present when mail from attorneys is inspected, have done all, and perhaps even more than the Constitution requires."[7]

Whether an inmate *must* be present is not decided, although some prison officials and most lower courts have required the presence of the inmate and have prohibited correctional officers from reading the mail.[8]

The official mail rules have been applied by courts to prisoner correspondence with the media in opinions that recognize the need for confidentiality of such communications.[9]

May prisoners correspond with legal assistance agencies?
Yes. Several courts have upheld the right of prisoners to correspond with legal assistance agencies, the American Civil Liberties Union, and with lawyers they had not previously retained on the ground that reasonable access to the courts is predicated—at least in some situations—on an opportunity to interest attorneys in taking the prisoner's case.[10] At least one federal court, the Court of Appeals for the Eighth Circuit, stipulated that prison officials may place reasonable restrictions on correspondence with the ACLU.[11] And in a somewhat analogous context, the Fourth Circuit Court of Appeals permitted a prisoner to write to *Playboy* magazine in an effort to raise money for his defense.

An important decision in this area has resulted from the efforts of inmates at Green Haven Prison in New York to organize a Prisoners' Labor Union. Several prisoners had written to the Prisoners' Rights Project of the New York Legal Aid Society requesting advice and assistance with respect to the formation of the union. Prison officials refused to recognize the union and withheld letters from the Legal Aid Society to prisoners at Green Haven. The Second Circuit Court of Appeals ordered the officials to deliver the letters, holding that they did not present a clear and present danger to the security of the institution. The court stated:

> Under the test for attorney-client mail, the state must show clearly an abuse of access in order to justify restriction. Defendants claim that such an abuse exists here, because the letter advocated an "unlawful scheme". . . .
> The contention that an application for recognition of the Union and communication with one's clients preparatory to such application are components of an unlawful scheme seems a misuse of that term. The lawyers were telling the prisoners to utilize lawful, not unlawful channels for the presentation of grievances and were guiding a challenge to a prison rule through orderly procedures. It is difficult to discern in what other fashion the prison would prefer to have the rule examined; it is the only peaceful method by which it can be reviewed by someone other than the Commissioner or his deputy. . . .[12]

Aside from legal correspondence, do prisoners have the right to correspond with whomever they choose?

No. Prisoners may not write whatever they please to whomever they please although it is clear that prison authorities no longer have total power to limit prisoners' correspondence.[13] At the very least, prison officials must provide a means by which mail may be sent and received by inmates. However, prisoner mail to and from the general public (family, friends, and the like) is subject to being opened and read by prison officials,[14] although several courts have ruled that outgoing general correspondence may not be opened, read, or censored.[15]

There are, however, specific limitations on the right of prison authorities to censor or withhold general correspondence. In *Procunier v. Martinez*, the Court ruled that inmate mail may be censored only if there is substantial evidence that the letter will jeopardize security, order, or rehabilitation. For example, a prison can censor a letter which includes escape plans. Going further, one court has said that the prison can seize a letter sent to a publisher to protest the fact that the publisher had not delivered certain books when the books would have been in violation of prison rules if they were delivered.[16] However, officials may not censor mail simply to eliminate unflattering opinions, factually inaccurate statements, or inflammatory racial, political, or religious views.[17]

In *Turner v. Safley*,[18] the Court sustained a regulation prohibiting correspondence between inmates of different institutions except when they are immediate family members or are writing concerning legal matters. The Court gave broad deference to the officials' exaggerated claims that such correspondence could foster escape attempts or could be used to facilitate the activities of prison gangs and rejected alternative means of protecting against such possible abuses (such as censoring mail) as too intrusive on prison management.[19]

Some prisons require that prior approval from the prison administration must be obtained by the inmate for each correspondent; others place a numerical limitation on the number of letters written. For the most part, however, the courts have properly struck down such rules.[20] The First Amendment also protects the person with whom the prisoner seeks to correspond; that person has a right to have letters delivered "free of unjustified interference."[21]

What procedures must be followed in censoring prisoners' mail?

In *Procunier v. Martinez*, the Court also required certain due process procedures which must be followed before a letter may be censored. A prisoner must be notified that such a letter has been rejected and must be given an opportunity to protest that decision. Further, any complaints must be referred to a prison official other than the person who originally disapproved the letter. Whether these procedures are in fact followed is, of course, open to question.

Would not uncensored correspondence create a security risk in prison?

No. The claim by administrators that censorship is necessary—even with respect to communications with the courts and legal counsel—rests on the theory that the mails might be used to transmit contraband, to plan escapes, or to engage in other unlawful schemes. The likelihood of any of these dire predictions becoming reality is very slim indeed. The experience in jurisdictions which permit an unlimited right to communication indicates that there is, in fact, no support for these fears.

This is particularly true with regard to official mail. Certainly, in view of the importance of the attorney-client relationship, the due process right of access to the courts, and the right of privacy, the minimal chance of abuse of the right to free communication is certainly outweighed by the constitutional rights of the prisoners.

Furthermore, allowing mail to be reviewed makes it difficult for prisoners to be able to report on prison conditions. Prisoners are often punished in one of the numerous low-visibility ways that prison officials employ in dealing with unpopular or rebellious prisoners when their communications consist of complaints to courts concerning prison conditions. Often, this punishment involves only an exercise of discretion and therefore cannot be a successful basis for any legal challenge to the official actions. Reading of mail may very well deter prisoners from exercising their right to communicate with the courts. If there is a fear that such communications will result in some form of retribution, it is likely that at least some prisoners will not risk the consequences. Several courts have held it to be unconstitutional for prison officials to impose or threaten to impose punishment based upon a prisoner's complaints to a court.[22]

Do prisoners have a right of access to the media?

In three opinions, the United States Supreme Court has considered access to the media through the use of interviews. Unfortunately, the opinions retreated from the point reached by some of the more progressive lower federal courts. In *Pell v. Procunier*,[23] the Court considered the constitutionality of regulations which prohibited face-to-face interviews between press representatives and the individual inmates whom they specifically name and request to interview. The Court held that as long as the regulation was applied neutrally, without regard to the content of the expression, it was valid since there were alternative avenues of communication—most notably, the mails—open to inmates who wanted to reach the press. Turning to the question of whether a prohibition of face-to-face interviews violated the rights of the press, the Court noted that it was sufficient that press people were allowed to talk to anyone they encountered while touring the institution. Also, the result of stopping face-to-face interviews left the press in the same position as the general public. The Court concluded that as long as the press had access to sources of information available to the general public, the right to freedom of the press was not abridged by this limitation.

Similarly, in *Saxbe v. Washington Post Company*,[24] the Court considered the constitutionality of a prohibition of all press interviews with designated prisoners. The Court again noted that there were other means to get information and that, with regard to interviews, the press was receiving the same treatment given the general public. Finally, in *Houchins v. KQED, Inc.*,[25] the Court again ruled against a media request for access to interview, photograph, and make recordings for publication, even though no other meaningful alternative existed for informing the public of prison conditions.

As a result of these cases, an inmate's right to communicate by mail with the media is made even more important. The leading case in this area is *Nolan v. Fitzpatrick*,[26] where the court held that prisoners have a right to send letters to the press concerning prison management, treatment of offenders, or personal grievances, except those which (1) contain or concern contraband or (2) contain or concern any plan of escape or device for evading prison regulations. The court found that the need for this right is "buttressed by the invisibility of prisons to the press and the public; the prisoners' right to speak is enhanced by the right of the public to hear." Under this ruling, prison officials may continue to open and read these communications, but only to determine if the inmate was adhering to the court's limitations.

Another court has gone even further and held that prisoner-media mail must be treated as official mail, i.e., outgoing mail cannot be opened and incoming mail can only be opened to check for contraband. The court justified its rule as follows:

> An informed public depends upon accurate, effective reporting by news media. In refusing to block inmate-press correspondence and in protecting it from censorship we protect not only the interest of the inmates, but that of the public at large, and we move the decisions related to

prison conditions out of the federal courthouse and into the public forum where they belong.[27]

In related developments, the correctional departments of numerous states, including New York, Pennsylvania, and Massachusetts and the Federal Bureau of Prisons, permit newsmen access to the prisons to interview willing prisoners.

Do prisoners have a right to read what they choose?

Despite some advances in recent years, prison officials continue to exercise a heavy hand of censorship on the kinds of books, magazines, and other reading materials that prisoners may possess and read. In some states, prisons maintain a list of approved publications for inmates, while in others the decision as to what books and magazines are legitimate is made on an ad hoc basis. All too often, prison officials attempt to censor controversial political, religious, or social books.

Cases challenging these overly restrictive policies have succeeded where the courts have required specific and substantial proof that prison discipline or security will be undermined by allowing inmates to read and possess material in question.

The courts have generally required prison officials to meet the same test for censorship of these materials as they must for censorship of correspondence.[28] This test, which is somewhat less demanding of prison officials than the "clear and present danger" test applicable to government attempts to repress free speech activity on the outside, places the burden on prison officials to demonstrate a substantial state interest centering around prison security or prison discipline *prior* to any censorship.

The areas in which the courts are most likely to uphold censorship involve writings or publications that are pornographic, obscene, or otherwise sexually oriented, those which detail the use or manufacture of explosives or weapons, or those which would aid in escape attempts. Where the material deals with political issues or criticism of prison conditions, most judges have struck down censorship attempts.[29]

Properly enforced, this standard can open prison doors to a wide range of materials that prison officials historically have suppressed. Most knowledgeable prison administrators and social scientists agree that that there is virtually no incident of

violence or disruption in prison that is caused by written publications. As Marvin Wolfgang, a leading criminologist, has
testified: "I know of no systematic, compelling or convincing
social science evidence that can link the kind of publications,
the kinds of reading matter or visual matter to which inmates
are exposed, to the degree of aggression or violence that is
found in prisons."

Despite the clear lack of proof of any causal connection between publication and security, prison officials refuse to give
up old myths and insist on their right to censorship. The courts'
record in this area is mixed. In one case, a New York State
prison had originally forbidden works by Arthur Koestler, Erik
Erikson, Charles Silberman, and George Jackson and had
banned *National Geographic* magazine. During the litigation
challenging this censorship, the prison agreed to allow all of
these books to be received by prisoners, as the court found no
"absolutely necessary" reason for this policy.

One of the earliest barriers to fall was the limitation on the
right of prisoners to receive black-oriented papers and magazines.[30] Martin Sostre, an outspoken black prisoner in New
York, litigated several facets of the "right to read" issue. The
Second Circuit Court of Appeals has held that he could not be
punished for possessing "inflammatory" and "racist" literature
but made it clear that he had no right to distribute the material
to other prisoners.[31]

A district court in New York partially vindicated Sostre's
rights in another case in the receipt of literature area. State
prison officials had withheld issues of the Black Panther newspaper, the *Workers World*, and several books including the
writings of Mao Tse-tung. At the time this material was withheld, no regulations existed to guide prison officials in determining whether to censor reading material. Nor were prisoners
provided the right to contest these decisions. The court ruled
that reading material could only be withheld if it posed a clear
and present danger to the security of a prison or to the rehabilitation of prisoners and further required that prior to censorship, the prisoner must be notified of the intent to censor,
be given some opportunity to object to the censorship, and be
provided with a decision by an impartial board applying constitutional standards.[32]

A federal district court in New York, employing the same

constitutional analysis, ordered that New York State prisoners have the right to receive *Fortune News*, the newsletter of the Fortune Society, an organization of former inmates which publishes articles and information on prison alternatives, exconvicts' rehabilitation, and other related subjects.[33] The court found that the mere assertion that the newsletter did not accurately reflect conditions in the prisons failed to show a compelling reason why it should be banned. In a sharp rebuke to those who would justify censorship in this context, Judge Weinfield stated:

> Free discussion of the problems of society is a cardinal principle of Americanism—it is part of our cherished heritage. Prison administration has been the subject of deep concern in contemporary society. Citizens, public groups, and officials, as well as inmates, have been sharply critical of our correctional and penal practices and procedures. Various sectors of the community have charged correctional and prison administrators, and the courts as well, with administrative deficiencies and policies. Whether justified or not, prime responsibility for these alleged shortcomings has been attributed by many, including newspapers, to the courts and prison administrators. However distasteful or annoyed or sensitive those criticized may be by what they consider unjust criticism, half truths or information, it does not justify a ban of the publication carrying the alleged offending comments. Censorship is utterly foreign to our way of life; it smacks of dictatorship. Correctional and prison authorities, no less than the courts, are not above criticism, and certainly they possess no power of censorship simply because they have the power of prison discipline.

An interesting example of the limited view that officials take of a prisoner's First Amendment rights and of a court's decisive stand against such censorship is found in *Abdul Wali v. Coughlin*.[34] In that case, the commissioner of the Department of Correctional Services in New York State had prohibited prisoners at Attica Prison from receiving a report prepared by Prisoner Legal Services of New York concerning the conditions at Attica. The report harshly condemned prison officials for their failure to respond to serious problems including guard brutality and racism. The commissioner justified his decision on the grounds that the report was inaccurate, inflammatory, and likely to cause disruptions at a "tense" institution. The Court ruled that the prisoners had a First Amendment right to receive the report, placing a high priority on the rights of prisoners to read a wide variety of materials and ruling that state censorship would be permitted only in the most compelling circumstances.

The problem of actually obtaining books, magazines, and other written materials has been aggravated by a rule in effect in many prisons allowing prisoners to receive these materials only from the original publisher. In 1979 the Supreme Court sustained a policy of the Federal Bureau of Prisons requiring all hardbound books to be sent directly from the publisher, citing security and administrative problems with regard to possible secreting of contraband if the books were delivered by family or friends.[35] Soft-covered or paperback books are permitted from any source under bureau regulations.

The courts have disagreed on a related subject: regulations that prohibit nude or seminude photographs.[36] At issue, of course, are the highly questionable, indeed preposterous claims of prison officials that these photographs and similar materials lead to sexual assaults and other disciplinary problems.

Do prisoners have a right to publish their own writing?

Restrictions exist also on an inmate's right to disseminate and publish his own written materials outside the prison. For example, the Federal Bureau of Prisons requires submission of all manuscripts to the warden prior to publication on the outside. This regulation has been upheld by a federal court in Connecticut in a case involving Daniel and Philip Berrigan, who had attempted to bypass the rule by sending sermons directly to outside contacts. The court rejected the argument that this regulation was an invalid restriction of their rights under the First Amendment.[37]

However, in determining whether an article may be censored, the same rules which apply to censorship of inmate mail apply to censorship of articles. Material written by prisoners may not be stopped unless it is likely to interfere with a legitimate governmental interest in security, order, or rehabilitation. For example, prohibition of an inmate newspaper may not be based on disagreement with its editorial comments.[38]

In an effort to prevent prisoners from gaining profits from their criminal acts, a number of states have enacted laws that designate royalties from books or articles about the prisoner's own case for the victim or a general victim's fund.

In an unusual case, the California Supreme Court has ruled that prisoners who write books that are published while they are incarcerated cannot be forced to contribute any part of their royalties to the prison administration.[39] The charge was supposedly for "handling costs," but the court found that prison censors were compensated by the state and that the prisoner-author was not benefited by this payment in any respect.

In a related area, the courts have ruled that regulations that totally bar written communications or exchange of materials between prisoners are unconstitutional. The prison must justify any such rule by showing a need to protect against escape attempts and other illegal plans.[40]

Do prisoners have a right to face-to-face interviews with lawyers and other legal persons?

Yes. Interviews with one's own attorney is a right, subject to restrictions on time, place, and manner of the interview.[41] An attorney-client interview may be restricted only under the most extraordinary conditions. For example, one court has held that where a prisoner's actions in segregation constituted a danger even to his counsel, the prison administrators had a duty to prohibit counsel from seeing his client until the situation changed.[42] In *Procunier v. Martinez,*[43] the right of an attorney to interview her client was extended to law students and para-professionals working for an attorney.

In addition, there is the right to confidential visitation. Courts have ordered prisons to provide adequate space, privacy, and ventilation for contact, confidential visits.[44] And where distance makes personal visitations difficult, the prison must afford reasonable telephone access between attorney and client.[45]

May prison authorities prohibit inmates from providing legal assistance to each other?

No. One of the most critical needs of a prisoner who has been convicted and sentenced is competent legal assistance if he desires to challenge his commitment. While the Constitution requires that counsel be appointed for those charged with a crime who cannot retain private lawyers, this right applies only to trials and direct appeals. Most states do not provide free counsel for inmates who institute postconviction proceedings, that is, attacks on their convictions and sentences after or in place of direct appeals. Prisoners are generally provided little or no guidance in determining whether they have grounds for a legal challenge, in preparing writs, and in litigating their cases. As a result, the practice of jailhouse lawyering has become widespread with some inmates providing counseling and drafting services for other prisoners.

Up until 1969, prisoners were punished for providing legal assistance to their fellow inmates. Then, in *Johnson v. Avery*,[46] the Supreme Court ruled that unless prison officials provide reasonable legal assistance to inmates, they may not prohibit prisoners from assisting each other with legal work. The Court found that the due process right to unimpeded access to the courts overrode any objection that prison officials made on the ground that jailhouse lawyers would interfere with prison discipline. The Supreme Court has reaffirmed this principle and has extended its application to habeas corpus petitions and civil rights actions.[47]

Do any legal assistance programs exist?

Many prisons have moved to implement the Supreme Court's directive by establishing legal assistance programs. These vary from prison to prison but generally incorporate the use of lawyers or law students to counsel and represent inmates in postconviction proceedings. Where such programs have not been instituted, courts have invalidated regulations prohibiting "legal practice" by jailhouse lawyers. In one case, where prisoners showed that the backlog of requests for legal assistance was so great that they had to wait for eighteen months to receive assistance from law students, the court permitted jailhouse counseling by inmates to continue.[48]

Other programs designed to meet the Supreme Court's mandate involve combinations of legal services programs, volunteer lawyer assistance, and law student research and assistance although student aid alone is not sufficient to satisfy the rights of inmates. Further, if a legal clinic exists, inmates must be allowed to use it to bring suit against the institution and its personnel unless reasonable alternatives are available.[49]

Are there any restrictions on jailhouse lawyers?

Notwithstanding the Supreme Court's rulings, some courts have upheld limitations on the jailhouse lawyer. First, the courts have upheld regulations that prohibit inmates from soliciting legal business and from demanding or receiving compensation for their services.[50] This is based on the fact that prison officials expressed concern that it is the general practice for prison lawyers to demand payment—whether it be in the form of cigarettes, money, or sexual favors—for their services and that by establishing a powerful subculture in the prison, they tend to undermine prison discipline.

Second, the courts have ruled that prisons may limit the time and place of jailhouse lawyering to prevent interruption of normal prison activities, so long as the right to counsel is not unreasonably impeded. But regulations that place complete discretion in any prison official to permit or prohibit inmate legal assistance at his option are clearly invalid. An example of a regulation likely to be upheld is one which prohibited a jailhouse lawyer from rendering legal assistance to someone outside the institution.[51]

Many prisons, even after the Supreme Court ruling, prohibited inmates from possessing another inmate's legal materials or papers in his cell, prohibited the use of typewriters, limited the number of legal books in the prison library and in individual cells, and limited the amount of paper and other material needed for effective representation.[52] However, the Supreme Court of California ruled that inmates may possess legal papers of other inmates since this is integral to effective counseling.[53] The court suggested that the prison had other ways of controlling abuses that may accompany the possession of other inmates' papers. Courts have generally upheld what they have considered to be reasonable limitations on paper, pens, pencils, and legal materials in cells on the grounds that they did not unduly interfere with counseling.

In *Bounds v. Smith*,[54] the Supreme Court ruled that the right to access to the courts required prison officials to provide all prisoners with adequate law libraries or adequate assistance from persons trained in the law. Previously, in *Younger v. Gilmore*,[55] the Court had required California to greatly expand its prison law libraries by affirming a lower court's ruling that:

> A prisoner should know the rules concerning venue, jurisdiction, exhaustion of remedies, and proper parties respondent. He should know which facts are legally significant, and merit presentation to the court, and which are irrelevant and confusing. . . . "Access to the courts", then, is a larger concept than that put forth by the State. It encompasses all the means a defendant or petitioner might require to get a fair hearing from the judiciary on all charges brought against him or grievances alleged by him.

Whether legal materials are necessary in a particular situation depends largely on whether there are adequate alternative means for access to the courts.[56] The burden of proving that these alternatives exist lies with the prison authorities.[57]

The courts have detailed what kinds of legal materials are necessary and have generally required a full complement of case reporters, statutes, and research materials.[58] Furthermore, prison officials must ensure adequate access to the law library. Supplying limited numbers of books to a cell, using a "paging" system, or denying access to prisoners in segregation are impermissible.[59]

The principal issue concerning law libraries and legal assistance is whether prison officials must provide anything more than an adequate law library. While the courts have not required the states to provide counsel,[60] some courts have insisted that some form of assistance be provided to illiterate prisoners. In one such case, the court ordered the prison to refrain from closing a prisoner-run clinic.[61]

The Supreme Court's opinion in *Bounds* affirms these principles. However, access to a complete law library and legal materials does not provide most prisoners with opportunities for judicial relief equal to that of inmates who are represented by counsel. Prisoners need a complete range of legal services.

NOTES

1. *Procunier v. Martinez*, 416 U.S. 396, 428, 94 S. Ct. 1800, 40 L. Ed. 2d 224 (1974).
2. *Id.* at 414.
3. *Turner v. Safley*, __U.S.__, 107 S. Ct. 2254, __L. __Ed. 2d__ (1987).
4. 312 U.S. 546, 61 S. Ct. 640, 85 L. Ed. 2d 1034 (1941).
5. *See, e.g., Guajardo v. Estelle*, 580 F.2d 748 (5th Cir. 1978); *Ruiz v. Estelle*, 679 F.2d 1115 (5th Cir. 1982); *Mawby v. Ambroyer*, 568 F. Supp. 245 (E.D. Mich. 1983); *Adams v. Carlson*, 488 F.2d 619 (7th Cir. 1973); *Smith v. Robbins*, 454 F.2d 696 (1st Cir. 1972).
6. 430 U.S. 817, 825–826, 97 S. Ct. 1491, 52 L. Ed. 2d 72 (1977).
7. 418 U.S. 539, 577, 94 S. Ct. 539, 41 L. Ed. 2d 935 (1974).
8. *Guajardo v. Estelle, supra* note 5; *Ruiz v. Estelle, supra* note 5; *Taylor v. Sterrett*, 532 F.2d 462 (5th Cir. 1976).
9. *Guajardo v. Estelle, supra* note 5; *Nolan v. Fitzpatrick*, 451 F.2d 545 (1st Cir. 1971).
10. *Davidson v. Scully*, 694 F.2d 50 (2d Cir. 1982).
11. *Burns v. Swenson*, 430 F.2d 771 (8th Cir. 1970).
12. *Goodwin v. Oswald*, 462 F.2d 1237 (2d Cir. 1972).
13. *Procunier v. Martinez, supra* note 1.
14. *See, e.g., Smith v. Shimp*, 562 F.2d 423 (7th Cir. 1977); *Feeley v. Sampson*, 570 F.2d 364 (1st Cir. 1978); *Guajardo v. Estelle, supra* note 5.
15. *Wolfish v. Levi*, 573 F.2d 118 (2d Cir. 1978), *rev'd on other grounds*, 441 U.S. 520, 99 S. Ct. 1861, 60 L. Ed. 2d 447 (1979); *Palmigiano v. Travisono*, 317 F. Supp. 776 (D.R.I. 1970); *Martino v. Carey*, 563 F. Supp. 984 (D. Or. 1983).
16. *McKinney v. DeBord*, 507 F.2d 501 (9th Cir. 1974).
17. *Procunier v. Martinez, supra* note 1, at 413; *Guajardo v. Estelle, supra* note 5.
18. *See supra* note 3.
19. *Id.* at 11–14.
20. *Guajardo v. Estelle, supra* note 5; *Gates v. Collier*, 501 F.2d 1291 (5th Cir. 1974).
21. *Trudeau v. Wyrick*, 713 F.2d 1360 (8th Cir. 1983).
22. *See, e.g., Carothers v. Follette*, 314 F. Supp. 1014 (S.D.N.Y. 1970), and *Haymes v. Montanye*, 547 F.2d 188 (2d Cir. 1976).
23. 417 U.S. 817, 94 S. Ct. 2800, 41 L. Ed. 2d 495 (1974).
24. 417 U.S. 843, 94 S. Ct. 2811, 41 L. Ed. 2d 514 (1974).
25. 438 U.S. 1, 98 S. Ct. 2588, 57 L. Ed. 2d 553 (1978). *Compare Main Road v. Aytch*, 522 F.2d 1080 (3d Cir. 1975) and 565 F.2d 54 (3d Cir. 1977).

26. *See supra* note 9.
27. *Guajardo v. Estelle, supra* note 5, at 759.
28. *See, e.g., Hopkins v. Collins,* 548 F.2d 503 (4th Cir. 1977); *Jackson v. Ward,* 458 F. Supp. 546 (W.D.N.Y. 1978).
29. *See, e.g., Jackson v. Ward, supra; Seale v. Manson,* 326 F. Supp. 1375 (D. Conn. 1971).
30. *Rowland v. Sigler,* 452 F.2d 1005 (8th Cir. 1971); *Jackson v. Godwin,* 400 F.2d 529 (5th Cir. 1968); *Sostre v. McGinnis,* 442 F.2d 178 (2d Cir. 1971).
31. *Sostre v. McGinnis, supra* note 29.
32. *Sostre v. Otis,* 330 F. Supp. 941 (S.D.N.Y. 1971).
33. *Fortune Society v. McGinnis,* 319 F. Supp. 901 (S.D.N.Y. 1970).
34. 754 F.2d 1015 (2d Cir. 1985).
35. *Bell v. Wolfish,* 441 U.S. 520, 99 S. Ct. 1861, 60 L. Ed. 2d 447 (1979). *Compare Spruytte v. Walters,* 753 F.2d 498 (6th Cir. 1985)(court enforces state rule allowing books to be sent by person other than publisher).
36. *See, e.g., Trapnell v. Riggsby,* 622 F.2d 290 (7th Cir. 1980); *Aikens v. Jenkins,* 534 F.2d 751 (7th Cir. 1976).
37. *Berrigan v. Norton,* 322 F. Supp. 46 (D. Conn. 1971).
38. *Luparar v. Stoneman,* 382 F. Supp. 495 (D. Vt. 1974). *But see Pittman v. Hutto,* 594 F.2d 407 (4th Cir. 1979).
39. *In re Van Geldern,* 5 Cal.3rd 832, 489 P.2d 578, 97 Cal. Rptr. 698 (1971).
40. *Rudolph v. Locke,* 594 F.2d 1076 (5th Cir. 1979).
41. *Souza v. Travisono,* 368 F. Supp. 959 (D.R.I. 1973), *aff'd in part,* 498 F.2d 1120 (1st Cir. 1974); *Cruz v. Beto,* 603 F.2d 1178 (5th Cir. 1979).
42. *Mims v. Shapp,* 399 F. Supp. 818 (W.D. Pa. 1975).
43. *See supra* note 1.
44. *Jones v. Wittenburg,* 509 F. Supp. 653 (N.D. Ohio 1980); *Nicholson v. Choctaw County,* 498 F. Supp. 295 (S.D. Ala. 1980); *Keker v. Procunier,* 398 F. Supp. 756 (E.D. Cal. 1975).
45. *Johnson v. Brelje,* 701 F.2d 1201 (7th Cir. 1983).
46. 393 U.S. 483, 89 S. Ct. 747, 21 L. Ed. 2d 718 (1969).
47. *See Wolff v. McDonnell, supra* note 7; *Buise v. Hudkins,* 584 F.2d 223 (7th Cir. 1978).
48. *Williams v. Department of Justice,* 433 F.2d 958 (5th Cir. 1970).
49. *Bryan v. Werner,* 516 F.2d 233 (3d Cir. 1975).
50. *McCarty v. Woodson,* 465 F.2d 822 (10th Cir. 1972).
51. *Heft v. Carlson,* 489 F.2d 268 (5th Cir. 1973); *Rizzo v. Zubrik,* 391 F. Supp. 1058 (S.D.N.Y. 1975).

52. *See, e.g., Conklin v. Wainwright,* 424 F.2d 516 (5th Cir. 1970); *McKinney v. Debord, supra* note 16.

53. *In re Harrell,* 2 Cal. 3d 675, 470 P.2d 640, 87 Cal. Rptr. 504 (1970).

54. *See supra* note 6.

55. 92 S. Ct. 250, 404 U.S. 15, 30 L. Ed. 2d 142.

56. *Cruz v. Hauck,* 627 F.2d 710, 721 (5th Cir. 1980); *Cody v. Hillard,* 599 F. Supp. 1025, 1060 (D.S.D. 1984).

57. *Johnson v. Anderson,* 370 F. Supp. 1373 (D. Del. 1974); *Russell v. Oliver,* 392 F. Supp. 470 (W.D. Va. 1975).

58. *Bounds v. Smith, supra* note 6, at 819–20, n. 4; *Wattson v. Olsen,* 660 F.2d 358 (8th Cir. 1981); *Cruz v. Hauck, supra; Sills v. Bureau of Prisons,* 761 F.2d 792 (D.C. Cir. 1985).

59. *Cepulonis v. Fair,* 732 F.2d 1336 (4th Cir. 1978); *Para-Professional Law Clinic v. Kane,* __F. Supp.__ (E.D. Pa. 1987); *Smith v. Bounds,* 610 F. Supp. 597 (E.D.N.C. 1985), *aff'd* 813 F.2d 1229 (4th Cir. 1987); *Johnson v. Anderson, supra* note 56; *McCray v. Sullivan,* 399 F. Supp. 271 (S.D. Ala. 1975).

60. *United States ex rel. Para-Professional Law Clinic v. Kane, supra* note 58; *Hooks v. Wainwright,* 775 F.2d 1433 (11th Cir. 1985).

61. *Para-Professional Law Clinic v. Kane, supra* note 58. *Also see Canterino v. Wilson,* 562 F. Supp. 106 (W.D. Ky. 1983); *Smith v. Bounds, supra* note 58; *Cody v. Hillard, supra* note 55.

IV
Political Rights

The essential political rights secured by the First Amendment—speech, association, assembly, and belief—have been given precious little breathing space in prison. The very nature of imprisonment has traditionally been held to require severe limitations on the right to assemble and associate with others. Mooveover, speech has been restricted whenever prison officials claim that it endangers prison security or discipline. And beliefs, though not as susceptible to manipulation or destruction by prison authorities, nevertheless have been effectively controlled by various forms of punishment—segregation, harassment, transfer, denial of parole, and so forth—which are often imposed on the prisoner who makes known his unpopular political beliefs.

Do prisoners have any political rights?

The regulation and restriction of political activities are not matters usually covered by written rules. Each particular assertion by a prisoner of his political right has been dealt with on an ad hoc basis, with individual decisions varying greatly not only from prison to prison but from inmate to inmate within a single institution. Therefore, it is impossible to advise prisoners of their political rights, at least in terms of what kinds of speech and other political activity may be tolerated at any given time in any prison. We are simply too far from a rule of law in prisons to be able to do that. This uncertainty has been heightened by the 1977 Supreme Court decision in *Jones v. North Carolina Prisoners Labor Union, Inc.*[1] At the very least, this case stands for the proposition that penal officials may bar solicitation by prisoners of other prisoners for membership in a prisoners' union, deny a union bulk mailing privileges, and bar union meetings. The prevention of group protest activities or organization of such activities that threaten security seems to be the primary result of the *Jones* case. Reconciliation of *Jones* with a First Amendment freedom of expression analysis in *Procunier v. Martinez*[2] is clearly a difficult proposition at the present time. The best approach is that *Martinez* "will continue to govern prison First Amendment challenges that focus on individual expression with the outside world, while *Jones* will be more often applied to group protest challenges."[3]

Can prisoners be punished for expressing their political beliefs?

The law is unclear. Several courts have held that First Amendment rights follow a person into prison and may be restricted only where their exercise creates a clear and present danger to the orderly administration of the institution. Unfortunately, however, the courts have generally subordinated First Amendment rights to the prison's determination of a speech or political activity's threat to prison discipline or security. Despite occasional flourishes of constitutional rhetoric stressing the importance of First Amendment rights for prisoners, the "hands-off" policy still has a secure grip in this area. The problem is further compounded by confusion surrounding the meaning of the *Jones* case.

With the changing and expanding nature of our prison population as well as economic dislocation looming, claims to political rights will in all probability be intensified in the future. While some may quarrel over the number of political prisoners in our institutions, there can be no doubt that blacks, Chicanos, and Native Americans—their numbers swelled by economic conditions—as well as inmates who are politicized as a result of their exposure to our correctional system will continue to push for the right to free political expression in prison.

The Second Circuit Court of Appeals' decision in the *Martin Sostre* case included a discussion of the right to political expression and beliefs.[4] Sostre had been punished by prison authorities for expressing "radical beliefs" in a letter to his sister and for collecting the writings of black nationalists and revolutionaries. In addition, he was punished for refusing to answer a warden's questions about the organization known as Republic of New Africa. The Court of Appeals ruled that this punishment was illegal since it "would permit prison authorities to manipulate and crush thoughts under the guise of regulation."[5]

In this context, at least one court has held that political discussions in an administrative segregation unit were a protected First Amendment activity, subject only to time (not after "lights out") and manner restrictions (no incitement or threats of incitement to disturbance).[6]

The courts have divided on the question of whether prisoners may draft and circulate petitions complaining about conditions in the prisons. In two cases, courts specifically ruled that the First Amendment protected such an activity, particularly if no maliciously false statements are made.[7] Other courts have cited a potential for abuse and coercion of nonsigners as a basis for denying this right.[8] The California Supreme Court has held that a ban on correspondence between a prisoner and a parolee (a prison union organizer) violates state statutes. The court found that the rule was based on opposition to the union and did not implicate any security interest of the prison administration.[9] This same court further permitted California prisoners to wear buttons and similarly rejected the security defense.[10]

Do prisoners have a right to associate with one another and to form political organizations?

The relative powerlessness of prisoners has led some to attempt to organize prisoner unions and political organizations. In California, a group called the United Prisoners' Union has drawn up a bill of rights for prisoners and is attempting to gain access to the prison populations with the hope, ultimately, of organizing the prisoners into the union. They publish a newspaper previously called *The Outlaw*, now the *Prisoners' Union Journal*. A leader in this movement has stated: "Until we unionize we are doomed eternally to the cruel cycle of poverty, prison, and parole and more poverty. In the widening class struggle we are the lowest of the low, denied the most basic constitutional rights and powerless to deal with an incredible opposition."

However, the idea of prisoners organizing and engaging in union activities was given harsh treatment by a majority of the Supreme Court in the *Jones* case. The decision, giving great deference to the asserted interests of the prison officials, stated that the fact of confinement and the needs of the penal institution impose limitations on constitutional rights, including those derived from the First Amendment.

Even prior to *Jones*, attempts by prisoners to form unions and to obtain certification as collective bargaining agents have

met with little success. A history of one such attempt at Green
Haven Prison in New York is illustrative of the practical and
legal problems. The organizing effort among the prisoners confined to this maximum-security facility fifty miles from New
York City began in the summer of 1971. Despite initial harassment and punishment by the administration, the movement
continued to grow. With the impetus of the Attica Prison re-
bellion of September 1971 and the assistance of lawyers from
the Prisoners' Rights Project of the Legal Aid Society of New
York City, which is counsel to the union, the movement finally
coalesced. A constitution was drafted and adopted in the late
fall of 1971, and authorization cards were circulated and signed
by the vast majority of the population. Simultaneously, a Public
Advisory Committee, comprised of labor leaders, liberal pol-
iticians, and public figures, was created to support the union.
Most significantly, the Prisoners' Labor Union also gained the
support and assistance of a strong, progressive labor union,
District 65, Distributive Workers of America, whose executive
committee authorized affiliation with the union, provided both
memberships ratified it.

In February 1972, the union, with a membership of 1300
out of a population of 1800, publicly announced its formation
and demanded recognition by the New York Department of
Correctional Services. Recognition was denied. The union then
filed a petition for certification as collective bargaining agent
for all the prisoners at Green Haven before the New York
Public Employment Relations Board. Since prisoners work for
the state and are paid for it, the Green Haven organization is
considered a public employees' union and as such is prohibited
under New York State law from striking.

Although certification was subsequently denied on the
grounds that the prisoners were not "public employees" within
the meaning of the state law,[11] one federal judge, in a case that
arose out of the organizing effort at Green Haven, wrote that
the Prisoners' Union was an idea whose day had come: "There
is nothing in federal or state constitutional or statutory law of
which I am aware that forbids prison inmates from seeking to
join, or correctional officials from electing to deal with, an
organization. . . .of inmates concerned with prison conditions
and inmate grievances."[12] This scenario was played out in Michigan with exactly the same results as in New York.[13]

Should prison officials be permitted to regulate inmate political activities?

No. It should be stressed, however, that these changes—as with most experiments of this nature—have caused resentment among officials who fear that prison discipline and security are jeopardized by reforms. The shift away from a strict security function has placed the correctional officers in a position to which they are not accustomed. This conflict will probably appear wherever changes in prison life lead to a significant decrease in the discretion and power of prison guards.

The indications are clear that, with few exceptions, prison authorities will not tolerate political organizing, and the *Jones* case has made any litigation with respect to union or organizing activities problematic. But just as the law changed with respect to unions and organizing on the outside with the advent of the depression and the Wagner Act, so the law can change in the future with changing circumstances within prisons.

Prison officials must not have unlimited discretion to permit or prohibit political activities. At the very least, these organizations should be protected unless prison authorities demonstrate that their existence or activities create a clear and present danger of subversion to legitimate prison administration. Officials should be required to adopt rules and regulations covering what activity will be subject to punishment; these rules must in turn be limited to prohibit only those activities which in fact pose a clear and present danger to prison security and discipline. Peaceful organizing, petitioning, meetings, advocacy, and assembly should be protected. Disagreement with political thought or speech cannot be valid grounds for a finding of clear and present danger; speech is always disruptive in that sense. Assembly in private by prisoners should only be prohibited on evidence, not mere speculation, of unlawful activity. And formation of organizations of inmates for the purpose of presenting unified demands or suggestions concerning prison life is essential to the prisoners' right to have some say in their day-to-day existence.

Are persons convicted of crimes entitled to vote?

The United States Supreme Court in *Richardson v. Ramirez*[14] permitted California to deny the right to vote to those persons convicted of felonies. That case makes the right to vote wholly dependent on each state's own laws. Disenfranchisement provisions may be located in state constitutions and statutes. To find out whether a person has lost the right to vote, consult Table 1, "State Disenfranchisement Provisions," located on pages 161–63 of David Rudenstine's *The Rights of Ex-Offenders* in the ACLU Handbook series.[15]

In *Hunter v. Underwood*,[16] the Supreme Court ruled unconstitutional a provision of the Alabama Constitution disenfranchising persons convicted of crime because it had been enacted with the intent of discriminating against blacks. In *Tate v. Collins*,[17] a district court upheld the right of Tennessee state prisoners to vote if not convicted of "infamous crimes" and ordered that prisoners be permitted to obtain absentee ballots.

Pretrial detainees, because they are merely awaiting trial and have not been convicted of a crime, should be entitled to the franchise. The Supreme Court has held that it is violative of the Equal Protection Clause of the Fourteenth Amendment for New York to deny absentee ballots to pretrial detainees.[18] Further, a consent decree filed in the United States District Court for the Eastern District of Pennsylvania in order to end a lawsuit brought by pretrial prisoners confined to Philadelphia jails would permit detainees to receive campaign literature, would permit such literature to be posted, and would permit access of candidates to the jail facilities.[19]

May prisoners receive visits?

All prisons allow visits by family members, and most allow visits by friends although the number and times for the visits are limited. Visits can be suspended for violation of visiting rules, but several courts have now held that visitors cannot be required to submit to strip searches unless the prison has some reasonable grounds to believe that the visitor is carrying contraband.[20]

There is no constitutional right to contact visits, even for pretrial detainees[21] although most institutions allow such visits.

NOTES

1. 433 U.S. 199, 97 S. Ct. 2532, 53 L. Ed. 2d 629 (1977).
2. 416 U.S. 396, 428, 94 S. Ct. 1800, 40 L. Ed. 2d 224 (1974).

3. Alexander, "The New Prison Administrators and the Court: New Directions in Prison Law," 56 Tex. L. R. 963, 1002–1003 (1978). Also compare *Guajardo v. Estelle*, 580 F.2d 748 (5th Cir. 1978) with *Preast v. Cox*, 628 F.2d 292 (4th Cir. 1980), and *Nickens v. White*, 461 F. Supp. 1158 (E.D. Mo. 1978), *aff'd* 622 F.2d 967 (8th Cir. 1980). *See Turner v. Safley*, __U.S.__, 107 S. Ct. 2254, __L. Ed. 2d__ (1987).

4. *Sostre v. McGinnis*, 442 F.2d 178 (2d Cir. 1971).

5. *Id. In U.S. ex rel. Larkins v. Oswald*, 510 F.2d 583 (2d Cir. 1975), the Court of Appeals for the Second Circuit upheld a jury verdict of $1,000 awarded to an Attica prisoner who was unlawfully punished, as Sostre was, for possessing "inflammatory" documents in his cell.

6. *Diamond v. Thompson*, 364 F. Supp. 659 (M.D. Ala. 1973). Compare *Lamar v. Coffield*, 353 F. Supp. 1081 (S.D. Tex. 1972)(prison officials could restrict speech to certain times and places to protect the safety and security of the prison) and *Evans v. Moseley* 455 F.2d 1084 (10th Cir. 1972)(inmates congregated outside associate warden's office to protest treatment in connection with attempt to form organization).

7. *Wolfel v. Bates*, 707 F.2d 932 (6th Cir. 1983); *Edwards v. White*, 501 F. Supp. 8 (M.D. Pa. 1979). *Also see Haymes v. Montanye*, 547 F.2d 188 (2d Cir. 1976) (transfer after circulating letter in yard and legal assistance activities held actionable); *Stovall v. Bennett*, 471 F. Supp. 1286 (M.D. Ala. 1979)(injunction entered against prison chaplain threatening Mormon prisoners who signed petition seeking rights).

8. *Adams v. Gunnell*, 729 F.2d 362 (5th Cir. 1984); *Nickens v. White*, *supra* note 3.

9. *In re Brant*, 25 Cal. 3d 136, 599 P.2d 89, 157 Cal. Rptr. 894 (Cal. S. Ct. 1979).

10. *In re Reynolds*, 25 Cal. 3d 122, 599 P.2d 86, 157 Cal. Rptr. 892 (1979).

11. *Matter of State of New York (Dep't. of Correctional Servs.) and the Prisoners' Labor Union at Green Haven*, Case No. C0794 (before the N.Y. Public Employees' Relations Bd., May 24, 1973). The adverse decision was upheld in *Matter of Prisoners' Labor Union v. Helsby*, 44 A.D.2d 707, 354 N.Y.S.2d 694 (N.Y. App. Div. 2d Dept. 1974), leave to appeal denied, 35 N.Y.2d 641 (1974).

12. *Goodwin v. Oswald*, 462 F.2d 1237 (2d Cir. 1972) (Oakes, J. concurring).

13. *Matter of the State of Michigan (Dep't. of Corrections) and Prisoners' Labor Union at Jackson, Michigan*, Case Nos. R72E-163, C72E-81, R72F-214, C72F-108 (proceedings before Michigan Public Employees' Relations Bd., Sept. 14, 1973 and March 19, 1974). The adverse decisions were upheld, *Prisoners' Labor Union at Marquette v. State Dep't. of Corrections*, 61 Mich. App. 328, 232 N.W.2d 699 (Mich. Ct. App. 1975). Also see *In re Price*, 25 Cal. 3d 448, 158 Cal. Rptr.

873, 600 P.2d 1330 (1979)(prisoners have no right to hold union meetings).

14. 418 U.S. 24, 94 S. Ct. 2655, 41 L. Ed. 2d 551 (1974). *See also Texas Supporters of WWP Presidential Candidates v. Strake,* 511 F. Supp. 149 (S.D. Tex. 1981).

15. At 167–170, Rudenstine has also provided a state-by-state list of constitutional and statutory citations concerning voting rights.

16. 471 U.S. 202, 105 S. Ct. 1916, 85 L. Ed. 2d 222 (1985).

17. 496 F. Supp. 205 (W.D. Tenn. 1980).

18. *O'Brien v. Skinner,* 414 U.S. 524, 94 S. Ct. 740, 38 L. Ed. 2d 702 (1974). *Also see Arlee v. Lucas,* 55 Mich. App. 340, 222 N.W.2d 233 (Mich. Ct. App. 1974). *But compare McDonald v. Bd. of Elections,* 394 U.S. 802, 89 S. Ct. 1401, 22 L. Ed. 2d 739 (1969)(not a denial of equal protection as other citizens are ineligable to receive absentee ballots).

19. *Prisoners Rights Council v. Aytch,* 2 PLM 37, No. 76-3311 (E.D. Pa. Apr. 16, 1979)(consent decree).

20. *Thorne v. Jones,* 765 F.2d 1270 (5th Cir. 1985); *Blackburn v. Snow,* 771 F.2d 556 (1st Cir. 1985).

21. *Block v. Rutherford,* 468 U.S. 576, 104 S. Ct. 3227, 82 L. Ed. 2d 438 (1984). Also see ch. 10.

V

Religious Rights and Discrimination

Under the First Amendment, all persons are guaranteed the right to the free exercise of their religious beliefs. Recognizing that this right is "preferred," that is, of particular significance under the Constitution, the courts have held that freedom of religion does not terminate at the prison door.

Are there any restrictions on the free exercise of religion by prisoners?

Yes. In *O'Lone v. Estate of Shabazz*,[1] the Supreme Court set forth a restrictive standard for federal court review of prisoner freedom of religion claims. In *O'Lone*, the Supreme Court held that prison policies do not violate a prisoner's religious rights if the policies are reasonably related to legitimate penological interests. The Supreme Court in *O'Lone* also stressed that federal courts must defer to prison officials' judgments. Although it is difficult to show that a prison policy that interferes with religion is not reasonably related to legitimate penological interests, it is not impossible. In a case handed down almost concurrently with *O'Lone*, the Supreme Court applied the same standard to strike down a policy that acted to bar most marriages of imprisoned individuals.[2]

While the *O'Lone* case suggests a court look at such issues as the availability of alternative means of exercising the remaining religious rights and the existence of possible accommodations to the exercise of religious rights, essentially the judgment of reasonableness is likely to be a subjective one, making it very difficult to predict the results of a particular case. It also means that plaintiffs in such cases should carefully prepare their cases to show how their religious practices can be accommodated without negative effect on prison security or rehabilitation, in order to show that restriction on religious freedom is an "exaggerated response" and thus invalid.[3]

Because *O'Lone* was decided just as this book went to press, cases in this chapter affirming religious rights must be viewed with considerable caution. Since they were decided before *O'Lone*, they may no longer be considered good law. Never-

theless, some religious rights are so well established in principle
that they are unlikely to be affected by this new decision. In
practice, members of orthodox religions generally have more
freedom to exercise their religious beliefs than other religious
groups since the practice of traditional beliefs is often not considered a threat to prison authority. Thus, prison staffs accommodate such religious expression. Most prisons allow possession
of the Bible, visits by and written communications with ministers of particular faiths, the receipt of religious materials, the
holding of religious services, and the wearing of religious medals and medallions. Indeed, traditional Christian worship is
encouraged in the belief that it reinforces conservative teach-
ings with regard to sin, repentance, and redemption.[4]

Cases involving traditional Christian faiths have most often
involved religious services for prisoners in segregated statuses,
and a majority of such challenges have been unsuccessful.[5] In
one of the two other prison cases involving religious rights to
reach the Supreme Court, the Court held that a Buddhist
prisoner must be afforded "a reasonable opportunity of pursuing
his faith comparable to the opportunity afforded fellow prisoners who adhere to conventional religious precepts."[6]

**Do Muslim prisoners receive the same protection as pris-
oners of other religions?**

Yes, in general. A large proportion of the early litigation over
the right to the free exercise of religion involved suits by Muslims. For the most part, Muslims requested the courts to grant
them the same rights the prisons had already afforded to members of other religious denominations. They asked, for example,
for their own bibles, religious reading material, religious services, and religiously acceptable diets—rights fairly well established for prisoners of other orthodox religions. In the First
Amendment area, Muslims were also instrumental in establishing new rights for prisoners of all religions. Any discussion
of the right to worship in prison inevitably revolves around
Muslims because both the content and practice of their religion
were once perceived as a threat to the administration of the
penal institution. Muslims developed close unity among themselves; prison officials had a morbid fear of any organized group
of inmates. Muslims, the majority of whom are black, did not
refrain from raising the issue of racism while prison officials

usually denied its very existence, much less its pervasiveness in prisons. Muslims were alienated from traditional prison procedures and practices (ranging from "rehabilitation" to diet); prison officials tend to view any prisoner or group that deviates from the prevailing model of corrections as a danger to the continuation of the closed prison society. As a result, prison administrators historically attempted to prevent Muslims from exercising their religion in the prisons, primarily through regulations and disciplinary punishment.

Given this background, the courts were faced with three basic issues in suits initiated by Muslims. The first was whether the various substantive rights requested, such as the right to possession of the Koran and the right to religious services in prison, are guaranteed by the First Amendment. The second was whether a prison discriminates against a particular variety of religious beliefs by permitting prisoners of some religions certain rights denied to Muslims. Finally, and of critical importance, the courts were called upon to rule on prison officials' claims that the various aspects of the practice of the Muslim religion in prison establishes a danger of substantial interference with the orderly functioning and discipline of the institution.

In more recent years, official hostility to Muslims has declined markedly in most prisons; many administrators either see Muslims as a stabilizing force in the prison population or have at least come to accept the basic legitimacy of the Muslim faith. Few prisons now bother to challenge the right of the Muslim faith to be recognized as a religion under the First Amendment, thereby guaranteeing to Muslim prisoners the same rights as other inmates to practice their religion.[7] The recognition of the Muslim faith was important as well for non-orthodox religions, members of which may sue to exercise their rights in prison.[8] As one court declared, even in prison a person has an absolute right to embrace the religious beliefs of his choice, and it is not the function of the court "to consider the merits or fallacies of a religion or to praise or condemn it, however excellent or fanatical or preposterous it may be."[9]

Similarly, the courts had little difficulty in ordering that Muslims have an absolute right to receive, possess, and read the Koran, the Muslim bible. The right to possess the Koran was granted either on the ground that the bibles of the major religious denominations are freely possessed by other prisoners or for the more basic reason that the constitutional guarantee to the free exercise of religion includes the right to read and study the religion's most important scriptures.[10]

Has the right of Muslims to practice their religion been restricted?

Yes. The first major dispute centered around the desire of Muslims to receive their newspaper, *Muhammed Speaks*, and to receive Elijah Muhammed's book, *Message to the Black Man in America*.

On this question, the courts split. Several sustained prison officials' arguments that the newspaper and book were inflammatory and racist and, therefore, a threat to prison order and discipline.[11] Several others ruled that Muslims have a right to receive these articles subject to censorship of offensive sections of the paper.[12] In recent years there has been little reported litigation on this issue, and apparently few prison systems still attempt to bar such literature. In *Mukmuk v. Commissioner of Dept. of Correctional Services*,[13] the court held that it is unconstitutional to punish a prisoner for possession of Muslim literature.

Walker v. Blackwell[14] holds that there is a constitutional right to correspond with Elijah Muhammed. While there are earlier decisions to the contrary, most courts would probably follow *Walker* today. Even the *Walker* court, however, upheld censorship of the communications as a reasonable limitation on the free exercise of religion.

Muslims have also challenged prison regulations forbidding or restricting their religious services in prison. Most penal institutions provide for religious services for the major religious denominations. These services, usually held once a week, are performed by a minister who is allowed access to the prison both for the services and for individual counseling and prayer. Most courts have recognized that the refusal to allow Muslims the right to religious services and religious counseling in the prisons while permitting it for other groups is an impermissible discrimination against religious beliefs. Accordingly, these courts have granted Muslims the right to collective worship and visitation by Muslim ministers.[15] However, as in *O'Lone*, considerations that amount to administrative convenience may restrict

the holding of Muslim religious services that occur on week-
days, rather than the traditional Saturday or Sunday sabbaths.
In a case prior to *O'Lone*, the Second Circuit remanded for a
hearing a claim by Muslims to a right to congregate for prayer
in the recreation yard.[16]

Most courts now require some limited recognition of a prisoner's religious name.[17] Muslims, however, cannot refuse frisks
by a guard of the opposite sex.[18]

**Must prison administrators make special provisions for the
dietary and other needs of Muslim and orthodox prisoners of
other religions?**

They must make reasonable provisions. Muslims have strongly
pressed their right to a pork-free diet as an integral part of
their religious beliefs and practices. Some courts have found
that there is sufficient pork-free food in the prison's diet to
sustain Muslims and have for that reason denied requests for
special food.

In one early case, several members of the Muslim faith alleged that their rights under the First Amendment had been
denied because prison administrators had refused to provide
them with a special diet and special feeding hours as required
by their religion. During the month of December (Ramadan),
Muslims require diets without pork and with Akbar coffee and
certain special pastries. In addition, this food must be eaten
after sunset. The prison officials provided Jewish inmates one
special meal a year at the time of Passover. The court discounted
this aspect of the argument on the ground that the Muslims
were asking for special privileges for a period of thirty days.
The court held that the added cost of the food, the expense of
preparation, and the additional security supervisors who would
be required to move the Muslims during the night hours outweighed "whatever constitutional deprivation petitioners may
claim."[19]

In other cases involving the dietary requirements of Muslims, different decisions have been reached. Prisoners in the
District of Columbia Jail brought a suit against jail administrators because a request for a minimum of one full-course,
pork-free meal per day had been denied. The petition went
on to plead release from confinement in the absence of compliance inasmuch as the resulting deprivation amounted to

cruel and unusual punishment. According to the court, the basic issue was "the degree to which officials of the District of Columbia Jail are constitutionally compelled to accommodate the dietary laws of the Muslim faith."[20] The court concluded that there was no reason why the use of pork as seasoning could not be reduced, why "non-pork substitutes for main dishes of pork" could not be provided, why menus showing pork content could not be posted in advance, and why pork dishes could not be more evenly dispersed throughout the meal cycle. The court stated:

> That penal as well as judicial authorities respond to con-
> stitutional duties is vastly important to society as well as
> the prisoner. Treatment that degrades the inmate, invades
> his privacy, and frustrates the ability to choose pursuits
> through which he can manifest himself and gain self-re-
> spect erodes the very foundations upon which he can pre-
> pare for a socially useful life. Religion in prison subserves
> the rehabilitative function by providing an area within
> which the inmate may reclaim his dignity and reassert his
> individuality. But, quite ironically, while government pro-
> vides prisoners with chapels, ministers, free sacred texts
> and symbols, there subsists a danger that prison personnel
> will demand from inmates the same obeisance in the re-
> ligious sphere that more rightfully they may require in
> other aspects of prison life. This danger is not chimerical.
> In recent years, against the directives of the District of
> Columbia Commissioners, Muslim inmates in the custody
> of the Department of Corrections have been deprived of
> the most basic religious liberties, which only by court order
> have been restored.[21]

Muslim prisoners have recently been generally successful in establishing a right not to be required to handle pork as part of their work assignments in violation of their religious beliefs.[22] In an important case, *Masjid Muhammed v. Keve*,[23] the pris-oners won preliminary relief consisting of the right to inspection of the institutional kitchen to assure that pork products were appropriately separated from food they consumed.

May prisoners wear religious symbols?
In general, the courts have upheld administrative bans on

the wearing of religious medals and head coverings upon a showing that such items pose a possible security threat.[24] However, if it can be shown that members of other religious groups can possess and wear similar medals or medallions, a strong equal protection claim can be made. In one significant case, again involving Muslim prisoners, it was shown that the District of Columbia Department of Corrections purchased, with public funds, religious medals for Catholic, Protestant, and Jewish inmates. The prisoners were allowed to keep these medals on their person and to wear them. No such medals were purchased for the Muslims nor could they be purchased anywhere within the prison. While attending instructions in Islamic culture, an inmate was given a Muslim religious medal. He wore the medal openly until it, along with all other Muslim medals in the prison, was confiscated. There was no indication that the medals of any other religion were confiscated. The court held that the confiscation of the medals was a violation of the prisoner's right not to be discriminated against because of his religion and that the prison administration must also provide Muslim medals from public funds as long as other medals were so provided.[25] Pretrial detainees have been granted greater rights in this area.[26]

May prisoners wear their hair in conformity with the beliefs and practices of their religion?

Probably. For some time, the trend has been favorable once sincerity of religious belief was established. A leading 1975 case, *Teterud v. Burns*,[27] held that a Native American prisoner had the right to refuse a haircut on the grounds of his adherence to his Native American religion.[28]

Do prisoners have the right to establish new religions or adhere to the beliefs of new religions?

Yes. If such beliefs are sincerely held by prisoners, they must be recognized by prison administrators and permitted to be practiced on the same basis as any traditional or previously established religion. This issue has been raised in cases involving the Church of the New Song. A Texas court has found that the Church of the New Song is not a religion protected by the First Amendment.[29] However, in a case arising in an Iowa state prison, the federal court reached a different result, finding that the Church of the New Song was a religion that was entitled to the protection of the First Amendment.[30] But even courts that have recognized Satanism as a religion have refused to recognize a right to possess religious objects such as candles, chalices, incense, and bells in prison cells.[31]

NOTES

1. __U.S.__, 107 S. Ct. 2400, __L. Ed. 2d__ (1987).

2. *Turner v. Safley*, __U.S.__, 107 S. Ct. 2254, __L. Ed. 2d__ (1987).

3. *Id.* at 2256, 2259–63.

4. Indeed, occasionally prisoners have challenged prison practices requiring them to form an involuntary audience for traditional religions within the institution. *See Campbell v. Cauthron*, 623 F.2d 503 (8th Cir. 1980).

5. *Otey v. Best*, 680 F.2d 1231 (8th Cir. 1982); *Sweet v. South Carolina Dep't. of Corrections*, 529 F.2d 854 (4th Cir. 1975); *LaReau v. MacDougall*, 473 F.2d 974 (2d Cir. 1972). *See also St. Claire v. Cuyler*, 634 F.2d 109 (3d Cir. 1980). But such cases cannot be dismissed without requiring some justification from prison authorities for barring a prisoner from religious services. *See Green v. White*, 605 F.2d 376 (8th Cir. 1979). For other cases involving traditional Christian religions, see *Caldwell v. Miller*, 790 F.2d 589 (7th Cir. 1986)(trial court erroneously decided on summary judgment that ban on group religious activities could continue); *O'Malley v. Brierley*, 477 F.2d 785 (3d Cir. 1973)(requiring trial court to hold a hearing on whether prison officials reasonably barred particular Catholic priests from holding services), and *Glenn v. Wilkinson*, 309 F. Supp. 411 (W.D. Mo. 1970)(prison ordered to make some location other than the shower room available for Catholic mass for prisoners in maximum security).

6. *Cruz v. Beto*, 405 U.S. 319, 92 S. Ct. 1079, 31 L. Ed. 2d 263 (1972). The other was *Cooper v. Pate*, 378 U.S. 546, 84 S. Ct. 1733, 12 L. Ed. 2d 1030 (1964), in which the Supreme Court held that claims that a prisoner was denied certain publications and denied other privileges solely on the grounds of his religious beliefs, stated a cause of action and could not be dismissed by the district court without a hearing.

7. *Sewell v. Pegelow*, 291 F.2d 196 (4th Cir. 1961); *Fulwood v. Clemmer*, 206 F. Supp. 370 (D. D.C. 1962); *Sostre v. McGinnis*, 334 F.2d 906 (2d Cir. 1964), *cert. denied*, 85 S. Ct. 168 (1964). For a good summary of the long battle in the New York State correctional system for recognition of the Muslim faith, see *Bryant v. McGinnis*, 463 F. Supp. 373 (W.D.N.Y. 1978).

8. Much of the litigation in more recent years has involved less well known religious groups, such as the Rastafarians.

9. *Fulwood v. Clemmer, supra,* note 7, at 373. *But see* discussion hereafter with respect to Church of the New Song cases.

10. *Walker v. Blackwell,* 411 F.2d 23 (5th Cir. 1969); *Long v. Parker,* 390 F.2d 816 (3d Cir. 1968), and *Pitts v. Knowles,* 339 F. Supp. 1183 (W.D. Wis. 1972), *aff'd* 478 F.2d 1405 (7th Cir. 1973).

11. *Knuckles v. Prasse,* 302 F. Supp. 1036 (E.D. Pa. 1969); *Abernathy v. Cunningham,* 393 F.2d 775 (4th Cir. 1968).

12. *Brown v. Peyton,* 437 F.2d 1228 (4th Cir. 1971); *Walker v. Blackwell, supra* note 10; *Northern v. Nelson,* 315 F. Supp. 687 (N.D. Cal. 1970).

13. 529 F.2d 272 (2d Cir. 1976), *cert. denied,* 96 S. Ct. 2238 (1976).

14. *See Walker v. Blackwell, supra* note 10. *See also Wiggins v. Sargent,* 753 F.2d 663 (8th Cir. 1985).

15. *See, e.g., Walker v. Blackwell, supra* note 10; *Long v. Parker, supra* note 10; *Cooper v. Pate,* 382 F.2d 518 (7th Cir. 1967); Courts have differed on the extent to which they have allowed variations for access to different religions under the Equal Protection Clause. *Compare Native American Council of Tribes v. Solem,* 691 F.2d 382 (8th Cir. 1982) with *Thompson v. Commonwealth of Ky.,* 712 F.2d 1078 (6th Cir. 1983).

16. *Aziz v. LeFevre,* 642 F.2d 1109 (2d Cir. 1981); *see also Cochran v. Rowe,* 438 F. Supp. 566 (N.D. Ill. 1977).

17. *Compare Imam Ali Abdullah Akbar v. Canney,* 634 F.2d 339 (6th Cir. 1980)(prison not required to recognize Muslim name) with *Masjid Muhammad-D.D.C. v. Keve,* 479 F. Supp. 1311 (D. Del. 1979)(prisoners can not be disciplined for failure to acknowledge names, other than religious names, but officials need not change their records); *Barrett v. Commonwealth of Va.,* 689 F.2d 498 (4th Cir. 1982)(statute denying recognition of prisoners' religious names violates First Amendment); *Azeez v. Fairman,* 604 F. Supp. 357 (C.D. Ill. 1985); and *Salahuddin v. Carlson,* 523 F. Supp. 314 (E.D. Va. 1981).

18. *Madyun v. Franzen,* 704 F.2d 954 (7th Cir. 1983).

19. *Walker v. Blackwell, supra* note 10.

20. *Barnett v. Rodgers,* 410 F.2d 995 (D.C. Cir. 1969). A similar case is *Ross v. Blackledge,* 477 F.2d 616 (4th Cir. 1973). *See also Moorish Science Temple of America v. Smith,* 693 F.2d 987 (2d Cir. 1982). Claims by religious Jews for a kosher diet have generally met with fairly favorable receptions by the courts. *See Kahane v. Carlson,* 527 F.2d 492 (2d Cir. 1975) and *Schlesinger v. Carlson,* 489 F. Supp. 612 (M.D. Pa. 1980). *In United States ex rel. Wolfish v. Levi,* 439 F. Supp. 114 (S.D.N.Y. 1977), *rev'd on other grounds sub nom. Bell v. Wolfish,* 441 U.S. 520, 99 S. Ct. 1861, 60 L. Ed. 2d 447 (1979), the court struck

down on equal protection grounds the failure to provide a pork-free diet to Muslim prisoners when kosher diets were provided to religious Jews.

21. *Barnett v. Rogers, supra* note 20, at 1002–3.

22. *See Chapman v. Pickett*, 586 F.2d 22 (7th Cir. 1978), *following remand,* 491 F. Supp. 967 (C.D. Ill. 1980); and *Kenner v. Phelps*, 605 F.2d 850 (5th Cir. 1979).

23. *See supra* note 17.

24. *See St. Claire v. Cuyler, supra* note 5 and *Rogers v. Scurr*, 676 F.2d 1211 (8th Cir. 1982). *But see Burgin v. Henderson*, 536 F.2d 501 (2d Cir. 1976)(trial court required to hold hearing on constitutionality of prison's denial to Muslim of right to wear prayer hat); and *Reinert v. Haas*, 585 F. Supp. 477 (S.D. Iowa 1984)(granting preliminary injunction permitting prisoner to wear religious headband).

25. *Fulwood v. Clemmer, supra* note 7.

26. *Collins v. Schoonfield*, 363 F. Supp. 1152 (D. Md. 1973); *Smith v. Sampson*, 349 F. Supp. 268 (D.N.H. 1972).

27. 522 F.2d 357 (8th Cir. 1975).

28. *See also Burgin v. Henderson, supra*, requiring a hearing on the justification for the prison's prohibition on beards as applied to Muslims. Other favorable cases include *Weaver v. Jago*, 675 F.2d 116 (6th Cir. 1982) and *Gallahan v. Hollyfield*, 516 F. Supp. 1004 (E.D. Va. 1981)(Cherokee Indian Sons of Jacob sect); *Wright v. Raines*, 457 F. Supp. 1082 (D. Kan. 1978)(Sikh); *Moskowitz v. Wilkinson*, 432 F. Supp. 947 (D. Conn. 1977)(Orthodox Jew); and *Maguire v. Wilkinson*, 405 F. Supp. 637 (D. Conn. 1975). *But see Furquan v. Georgia State Bd. of Offender Rehabilitation*, 554 F. Supp. 873 (N.D. Ga. 1982).

29. *Theriault v. Silber*, 453 F. Supp. 254 (W.D. Tex. 1978).

30. *Remmers v. Brewer*, 361 F. Supp. 537 (S.D. Iowa 1973), *aff'd* 494 F.2d 1277 (8th Cir. 1974), *cert denied* 419 U.S. 1012 (1974). *See also Loney v. Scurr*, 474 F. Supp. 1186 (S.D. Iowa 1979).

31. *See Dettmer v. Landon*, 799 F.2d 929 (4th Cir. 1986); *cf. Childs v. Duckworth*, 705 F.2d 915 (7th Cir. 1983)(denying religious objects without reaching whether Satanism is a religion). *But see Kennedy v. Meacham*, 540 F.2d 1057 (10th Cir. 1976)(remanding to determine if Satanist adherents had a right to possess religious objects in their cells). *See also Jones v. Bradley*, 590 F.2d 294 (9th Cir. 1979)(even if Universal Life Church is a religion, inmate minister had no right to use chapel without outside sponsor or to proclaim marriages). In *Brown v. Johnson*, 743 F.2d 408 (6th Cir. 1984), a church identified with gay rights was barred from congregate services.

VI
Racial Discrimination

Is racial discrimination permitted in prison?
No. Following decisions by the United States Supreme Court invalidating various forms of racial discrimination outside of prison, the Supreme Court also has held that racial discrimination is likewise unconstitutional in prisons.[1] Prison officials may justify racial segregation only on a temporary basis in isolated instances when an emergency exists, and racially motivated violence is imminent.[2] Prison officials may not segregate prisoners by race based on a "generalized expectation of racial violence" or past racial tensions.[3] Similarly, prison officials may not justify racially segregated facilities by arguing that prisoners want such segregation.[4]

What forms does racial discrimination take in prisons?
There is racial discrimination in the assignment to housing units. The courts have held that prison officials may not have separate housing units for prisoners based on race.[5] Prison officials also may not assign prisoners to multi-person cells on the basis of race, even if these assignments are made in the reception process for incoming prisoners.[6] Prison officials may not concentrate Caucasian prisoners in one unit if they are in the minority in the prison.[7]

There is racial discrimination in the assignment to prison jobs. Courts have held that prison officials may not discriminate in the assignment of jobs. Prisoners of color may not be refused jobs because of their race or given only the menial jobs (such as porters) while Caucasian prisoners are assigned to the higher status jobs (such as clerks) and industry positions.[8]

There is racial discrimination in the assignment to segregation. Prison officials may not discriminate in the assignment to segregation units. Courts have found that prison officials were discriminating against black prisoners when evidence showed that black prisoners were disproportionately overrepresented in punitive segregation units and that they were the overwhelming majority punished for "insubordination."[9]

Can a court award damages for racial discrimination?

Yes. Courts have awarded damages for racial discrimination. In one case a federal district court awarded over $1400 to a black prisoner after finding that he had been demoted in his job assignment and had received a severe reduction in pay because of his race.[10] Another case awarded a black prisoner damages after finding that he had been subjected to racial segregation within the city jail.[11]

Can a court order an increase in staff from other racial groups?

Yes. The federal courts can order an increase in the numbers of staff from underrepresented racial groups if they find that prisoners of color have been discriminated against by a staff which is overwhelmingly Caucasian.[12] But a court may find that prisoners do not have the standing to litigate the issue of racially discriminatory practices in the recruitment and hiring of staff.[13]

How does one prove racial discrimination?

The Supreme Court in *Washington v. Davis*[14] held that disproportionate impact was not sufficient to prove racial discrimination, there must be proof of intent to discriminate. In some instances, however, discriminatory intent can be inferred from disproportionate impact where the difference is difficult to explain on nonracial grounds.[15] To prove racial discrimination in prison, therefore, evidence such as the following must be gathered:

1. Statistics showing that prisoners of color are assigned to punitive segregation or more menial jobs in proportions greater than their proportions within the prison population. This must be combined with some other evidence of racially demeaning treatment, such as the use of racial slurs or other statements by persons responsible for making these assignments which indicate that they have a racially stereotypic or demeaning attitude toward prisoners of color, e.g., "blacks are more aggressive than Caucasians" or "blacks are afraid of electricity."

2. Statistics which show a glaring disparity in the assignments to segregation and jobs, e.g., no prisoners of color assigned to any jobs or any jobs other than janitorial jobs; 95 percent of the prisoners assigned to punitive segregation over the past year are prisoners of color when they represent only 60 percent of the prison population. After the decision in *McCleskey v.*

Kemp,[16] some other evidence, like that described in number 1 above, should be added to support the conclusion that discrimination is taking place in the disciplinary system.

3. A policy which says that the races should be separated or that prisoners of color should not be assigned to a certain job or should be assigned only in limited numbers.

4. Any examples of differences in treatment between prisoners of color and white prisoners whose situations are similar, e.g., two prisoners of similar skills applied for a job but it was assigned to the white prisoner regardless of who applied first; same conduct yet a prisoner of color was charged with a disciplinary infraction while a white prisoner was not charged; same disciplinary infraction and similar disciplinary record yet the punishment is greater for the prisoner of color.

What can a prisoner do about racial discrimination?

Differences in treatment among prisoners may not always be due to racial discrimination. Therefore, a prisoner who suspects he or she has been discriminated against because of race should obtain as much information as possible about the situation, e.g., did the other prisoner have the same skills and were special skills required; did the other prisoner apply for the job before, at the same time, or afterward; did the other prisoner who did not get an infraction do the same thing in the eyesight or earshot of the staff person giving the infraction; was the other prisoner found guilty of the same infraction yet given a less severe punishment despite similar disciplinary records. In addition, the prisoner should file a grievance on any incident which may be an example of discrimination and maintain copies of the grievance and response. If there is evidence of a pattern of racial discrimination which the prison officials refuse to correct after being given notice of this, a lawsuit may be filed.

NOTES

1. *Washington v. Lee,* 263 F. Supp. 327 (M.D. Ala. 1966), *aff'd sub nom. Lee v. Washington,* 390 U.S. 333, 88 S. Ct. 994, 19 L. Ed. 2d 1212 (1968); *Cruz v. Beto,* 405 U.S. 319, 321, 92 S. Ct. 1079, 1081, 31 L. Ed. 2d 263 (1972).

2. *United States v. Wyandotte County, Kansas,* 480 F.2d 969 (10th Cir. 1973), *cert. denied,* 414 U.S. 1068 (1973).

3. *Mickens v. Winston,* 462 F. Supp. 910, 912 (E.D. Va. 1978), *aff'd* 609 F.2d 508 (4th Cir. 1979); *McClelland v. Sigler,* 327 F. Supp. 829 (D. Neb. 1971), *aff'd* 456 F.2d 1266 (8th Cir. 1972).

4. *Jones v. Diamond,* 636 F.2d 1364, 1373 (5th Cir. 1981)("In prisons, where hostility of every kind is rampant, freedom of choice is but a gauze for discrimination. . . ."); *Rentfrow v. Carter,* 296 F. Supp. 301 (N.D. Ga. 1968).

5. *Lee v. Washington, supra* note 1; *Berch v. Stahl,* 373 F. Supp. 412 (W.D.N.C. 1974); *Gates v. Collier,* 349 F. Supp. 881 (N.D. Miss. 1972); *Lamar v. Kern,* 349 F. Supp. 222 (S.D. Tex. 1972); *McLelland v. Sigler,* 327 F. Supp. 829 (D. Neb. 1971), *aff'd* 456 F.2d 1266 (8th Cir. 1972); *United States v. Wyandotte County, Kansas, supra* note 2.

6. *Blevins v. Brew,* 593 F. Supp. 245 (W.D. Wis. 1984); *Stewart v. Rhodes,* 473 F. Supp. 1185 (S.D. Ohio 1979).

7. *Mickens v. Winston, supra* note 3.

8. *Finney v. Arkansas Bd. of Corrections,* 505 F. 2d 194 (8th Cir. 1974); *Battle v. Anderson,* 376 F. Supp. 402 (E.D. Okla. 1974); *Gates v. Collier, supra* note 5.

9. *McCray v. Bennett,* 467 F. Supp. 187 (M.D. Ala. 1978). Other courts have also found discrimination in the assignment to punitive segregation by finding disproportionate impact on black prisoners in disciplinary proceedings. *Battle v. Anderson,* 376 F. Supp. at 410 and *Gates v. Collier,* 349 F. Supp at 887 (black prisoners subjected to greater punishment or more severe discipline than Caucasian prisoners for similar infractions).

10. *U.S. ex rel. Motley v. Rundle,* 340 F. Supp. 807 (E.D. Pa. 1972).

11. *Mickens v. Winston, supra* note 3.

12. *Pugh v. Locke,* 406 F. Supp. 318 (M.D. Ala. 1976); *Holt v. Hutto,* 363 F. Supp. 194, 205 (E.D. Ark. 1973) *aff'd and remanded in relevant part, Finney v. Arkansas Bd. of Corrections,* 505 F.2d 194, 210 (8th Cir. 1974)(ordering the district court to amend its decree to require an affirmative action program); *Battle v. Anderson, supra* note 8. In *Gates v. Collier, supra* note 5 at 887, 901; the court found that the defendants had previously only hired Caucasian staff and ordered them to stop engaging in racial discrimination in the recruiting and hiring of staff. *See also, Taylor v. Perini,* 431 F. Supp. 566, 692 (N.D. Ohio 1977)(requiring a plan for prescreening of candidates for correctional officer positions for racial bias). Parties have also entered consent agreements, agreeing to training of staff in race relations as well as affirmative action in hiring of staff. *See, e.g., Taylor v. Perini,* 455 F.

Supp. 1241, 1250 (N.D. Ohio 1978)(requiring human relations training of staff); *Finney v. Mabry,* 458 F. Supp. 720 (E.D. Ark. 1978)(requiring affirmative action hiring program); and *Kendrick v. Bland,* 541 F. Supp. 21, 37–38 (W.D. Ky. 1981)(requiring affirmative action hiring program).

13. *Wilson v. Kelly,* 294 F. Supp. 1005 (N.D. Ga. 1968).
14. 426 U.S. 229, 96 S. Ct. 2040, 48 L. Ed. 2d 597 (1976).
15. *Id.* at 240–43.
16. __U.S.__, 107 S. Ct. 1756, __ L. Ed. 2d__ (1987).

VII
Privacy and Personal Appearance

Prisoners have shown increasing interest in changing prison policy which currently restricts their rights to freedom of dress, personal appearance, and privacy.

Most prison officials insist that the right to privacy ceases to exist upon entry into the penal institution. For the most part the courts have agreed with prison officials. However, despite many setbacks, there is some recognition in the law that certain extreme invasions of a prisoner's privacy are unjustified.

Do prison authorities have the right to search inmates' cells?
Yes. In *Bell v. Wolfish*,[1] the Supreme Court said that a pretrial detainee has no reasonable expectation of privacy. But even if he retains some expectation, "no one can rationally doubt that room searches represent an appropriate security measure. . . .And even the most zealous advocate of prisoners' rights would not suggest that a warrant is required to conduct such searches. Detainees' drawers, beds, and personal items may be searched. . . ."[2] In *Hudson v. Palmer,* the Supreme Court went further and held that "the Fourth Amendment proscription against unreasonable searches does not apply within the confines of the prison cell."[3] Also in *Bell*, the Supreme Court then held that jail officials are not required to conduct cell searches in the presence of the inmates whose cells are searched.[4] However, that case does not preclude recognition of other inmate rights in the conduct of cell searches.[5] First, the Supreme Court did not review the holding of the Second Circuit that prisoners were to be given receipts for items seized from their cells.[6] And prison officials cannot intentionally and unnecessarily destroy prisoner property in the course of a cell search or intentionally take property during cell searches that is not prohibited as contraband by prison rules.[7] In addition, some courts recognize that certain kinds of prisoner property, such as private diaries and letters to attorneys, may not be seized and read during routine cell searches.[8]

Do prison officials have the right to conduct strip searches?

Under many circumstances, yes. Again, *Bell v. Wolfish* has limited the challenges that prisoners can raise in this area. In *Bell,* the Supreme Court held that jail officials could require inmates to submit to a visual body cavity search (a search in which the prisoner removes all his clothing, bends over, spreads his buttocks, and exposes his genitals) after contact visits. Despite the major invasion of privacy that *Bell* approves, some limits still exist. In particular, *Bell* states that "searches must be conducted in a reasonable manner."[9] For example, the decision does not approve searches in which guards make derogatory remarks to prisoners.[10] Nor does it preclude a challenge to body cavity searches conducted in the presence of correctional officers of the opposite sex, unless their presence is essential.[11] When a prisoner has not had contact with outsiders or other prisoners, courts have suggested that there is no justification for a visual body cavity search.[12]

The search in *Bell* did not involve any touching of the prisoner by the correctional officer involved. The law on the conduct of body cavity searches which involve a touching of the prisoners' genitals is not well settled. *United States v. Lilly*[13] holds that the prison officials bear the burden of proving the reasonableness of manual body cavity searches. In order to justify a random body cavity search of a prisoner returning from a furlough, the prison needs to show that the prisoner had notice that going on the furlough would subject the prisoner to the possibility of such a search. If the prison has reason to believe that the prisoner has contraband in a body cavity, however, no prior notice is necessary.[14]

There is another circumstance in which strip searches can be challenged. Jails cannot have an indiscriminate policy of strip searching individuals arrested on certain kinds of minor offenses not associated with the possession of contraband.[15]

Finally, the law is unsettled regarding the ability of prison officials to demand that visitors submit to a strip search or be denied the right to visit.[16]

Must correctional officers be of the same sex as the prisoners they guard?

Only if the guards' duties necessarily require them as a matter of everyday occurrence to observe prisoners undressed. Whenever possible, the courts hold, the prisoners' interests in privacy should be recognized without sacrificing both sexes' work opportunities. Thus, in *Forts v. Ward*,[17] for example, the court held that female prisoners' privacy interests could be satisfied by issuing them suitable nightwear and allowing prisoners to cover their cell observation windows for fifteen minute periods.[18]

Do prisoners have the right to control their personal appearance?

Traditionally, no. However, the familiar scene of prisoners dressed identically in gray garb, short haircuts, with no mustaches or beards is changing although at a fairly slow pace. The changes may have more to do with changing styles and tastes in the free society than with anything else. The changes themselves are relatively insignificant given their purpose. For instance, in New York, although prisoners no longer wear gray uniforms, they are now required to wear forest green work clothes. In some institutions mustaches are permitted but may only be grown on the upper lip and cannot extend below the corners of the mouth. Often supported by prison officials as necessary health and safety measures, grooming codes in reality deprive the inmate of his sense of identity and presence and enforce regimentation in the prison. Erving Goffman, in his *Essays on Asylums*, describes the "mortification" which prisoners are forced to undergo. One aspect of this process is the personal defacement of inmates by the prison:

> On admission to a total institution. . . . the individual is likely to be stripped of his usual appearance and of the equipment and services by which he maintains it, thus suffering a personal defacement. Clothing, combs, needle and thread, cosmetics, towels, soap, shaving sets, bathing facilities—all these may be taken away or denied him, although some may be kept in inaccessible storage, to be returned if and when he leaves.[19]

Have any changes taken place?

Little progress has been made in attempting to change this process. A number of states now allow prisoners to wear clothes other than institutionally issued material. Other aspects of personal appearance are also subject to suppression at the say-so of prison officials. Jewelry, artifacts, and other personal items are allowed only by permission. In a case involving Erika Huggins, a federal court in Connecticut ruled that where a prison regulation limited the jewelry women prisoners might wear to a wristwatch, earrings, a ring, and a necklace with a religious medal on it, no infringement of any constitutional rights existed.[20] Both prison administrators and the courts must be pushed on this issue and be made to recognize that dehumanization by forced conformity is a dangerous reality in our prisons.

With respect to physical appearance, the issue most frequently raised concerns the right of male prisoners to have long hair, beards, and mustaches. In one case, Bobby Seale, while awaiting trial in Connecticut, sued to vindicate his right to retain his beard. Prison officials sought to justify the prohibition against beards by citing them as a potential health hazard in the spread of lice among prisoners, but the court found there to be no problem of lice at the jail and ruled that Seale could wear his short beard and goatee.[21]

Most courts, however, have denied requests that prisoners be allowed to determine the length of their hair or to wear beards or mustaches.[22] They have stated that prison regulations in this regard are neither arbitrary nor harsh, and are supported by reasons of health (presumably long hair leads to health problems for men but not women) and the need to be able to identify prisoners. Some courts have in fact suggested that all men look alike in long hair and beards.[23] In *Hill v. Estelle*,[10] the court rejected an argument that there was an equal protection violation in the application of different hair rules to men and women. But a First Amendment religious liberty argument has been successful with respect to personal appearance. The Eighth Circuit has established the right of a Native American prisoner to refuse a haircut on the grounds of his religious principles.[25]

The whole process of cutting inmates' hair really amounts to a grisly flashback into an age when it was a recognized, acceptable practice of our penal institutions to disfigure the prisoner in some fashion so as to mark him—at least for some period of time—to be held up to scorn by the public at large. This was an attempt not only to deter others, but to break down the offender to an acceptable level of subserviency. During the early development of our legal system, the cutting off of ears, fingers, or other appendages of the inmate was sanctioned. Even after the sentence had been completed, society would know that this particular individual had been condemned. Our legal system in its more dreary past also sanctioned the cutting of hair as one method of placing the prison mark on the inmate. This was particularly true of women convicted of prostitution who were turned out into the street bald so that all would know they had been punished under the law.

Do prison officials have the right to deny an inmate's request to marry?

Only under very limited circumstances. In *Turner v. Safley,* the Supreme Court held recently that an inmate has a constitutional right to marry.[26] The Court went on to state that "[n]o doubt legitimate security concerns may require placing reasonable restrictions upon an inmate's right to marry, and may justify requiring approval of the superintendent."[27] As an example of a reasonable restriction, the Court cited its earlier ruling upholding a state's prohibition on marriage of inmates sentenced to life imprisonment.[28]

In *Turner,* the state regulation allowed an inmate to marry only if there existed compelling reasons to do so such as a pregnancy or the birth of an illegitimate child. The Court applied the "reasonable relationship" standard and held it was both impermissibly burdensome on the inmate's constitutional right to marry and an exaggerated response to legitimate penological objectives.[29] The Court stated that prison officials may regulate the time and circumstances under which the marriage ceremony itself takes place.[30]

NOTES

1. 441 U.S. 520, 99 S. Ct. 1861, 60 L. Ed. 2d 447 (1979)(no Fourth Amendment protection against cell search). *Cf. Block v. Rutherford,* 468 U.S. 576, 591, 104 S. Ct. 3227, 82 L. Ed. 2d 438 (1984)(Due Process Clause does not protect against cell seizure of inmate's property).
2. *Bell v. Wolfish, supra* note 1, at 557.
3. 468 U.S. 517, 526, 104 S. Ct. 3194, 82 L. Ed. 2d 393 (1984).
4. *Bell v. Wolfish, supra* note 1, at 555–57. *See also Block v. Rutherford, supra* note 1.

68 *The Rights of Prisoners*

5. In *Block v. Rutherford*, the Supreme Court held that the Fourth Amendment proscription against unreasonable seizure and destruction of property is inapplicable in a prison cell. However, the Court stated that this "does not mean that an inmate's property can be destroyed with impunity." 468 U.S. at 529, n.9 and 530–36 (remedy for destruction of property by prison officials exists under Due Process Clause if no adequate state remedy exists).

6. *Wolfish v. Levi*, 573 F.2d 118, 131–132, n.29 (2d Cir. 1978), *rev'd on other grounds sub nom. Bell v. Wolfish, supra* note 1. *See also Steinberg v. Taylor*, 500 F. Supp. 477 (D. Conn. 1980).

7. *See O'Conner v. Keller*, 510 F. Supp. 1359 (D. Md. 1981)(prisoner retains due process rights that his personal property not be unjustifiably confiscated). *Cf. Hudson v. Palmer, supra* note 3 (intentional deprivation of property by prison officials violates Due Process Clause if adequate state remedy does not exist).

8. For a discussion of these rights see *United States v. Hinckley*, 672 F.2d 115 (D.C. Cir. 1982); *Diguiseppe v. Ward*, 514 F. Supp. 503 (S.D.N.Y. 1981); *O'Conner v. Keller, supra* note 7, at 1368. *But see United States v. Vallez*, 653 F.2d 403 (9th Cir. 1981)(reading of letter in partially sealed envelope approved as reasonable search).

9. *Bell v. Wolfish, supra* note 1, at 560.

10. *See Massey v. Wilson*, 484 F. Supp. 1332 (D. Colo. 1980).

11. *See Lee v. Downs*, 641 F.2d 1117 (4th Cir. 1981).

12. *See Bono v. Saxbe*, 620 F.2d 609 (7th Cir. 1980), and *Ruiz v. Estelle*, 503 F. Supp. 1265 (S.D. Tex. 1980). *Also see Bell v. Wolfish, supra* note 1, at 559, n.40.

13. 576 F.2d 1240 (5th Cir. 1978). *Cf. Bell v. Wolfish, supra* note 1, at 558–60.

14. *See Lee v. Downs, supra* note 11.

15. *See Logan v. Shealy*, 660 F.2d 1007 (4th Cir. 1981)(arrest for drunk driving; detainee not mingled with general jail population) and *Tinetti v. Wittke*, 620 F.2d 160 (7th Cir. 1980)(minor traffic offenses).

16. *See, e.g., Thorne v. Jones*, 765 F.2d 1270 (5th Cir. 1985)(decision to require visitors to submit to strip search as a condition of contact visiting was subject only to review for reasonableness); *Toussaint v. McCarthy*, 597 F. Supp. 1388 (N.D. Cal. 1984); *Wool v. Hogan*, 505 F. Supp. 928 (D. Vt. 1981)(upholding right of prison officials to require strip search of girlfriend). *But see Blackburn v. Snow*, 771 F.2d 556 (1st Cir. 1985); *Hunter v. Auger*, 672 F.2d 668 (10th Cir. 1984).

17. 621 F.2d 1210 (2d Cir. 1980).

18. *See Bowling v. Enomoto*, 514 F. Supp. 201 (N.D. Cal. 1981); *Hudson v. Goodlander*, 494 F. Supp. 890 (D. Md. 1980); *Gunther v. Iowa*

State Men's Reformatory, 462 F. Supp. 952 (N.D. Iowa 1979). *Also see* ch. 8.

19. Goffman, *Essays on Asylums,* at 20 (Anchor Books, 1961).

20. *Seale v. Manson,* 326 F. Supp. 1375 (D. Conn. 1971).

21. *Id. But see Blake v. Pryse,* 444 F.2d 218 (8th Cir. 1971) and *Rinehart v. Brewer,* 360 F. Supp. 105 (S.D. Iowa 1973), *aff'd* 491 F.2d 705 (8th Cir. 1974).

22. *See Phillips v. Coughlin,* 586 F. Supp. 1281 (S.D.N.Y. 1984); *Sloan v. Southampton Correctional Center,* 476 F. Supp. 196 (E.D. Va. 1979); *Poe v. Werner,* 386 F. Supp. 1014 (M.D. Pa. 1974).

23. Some early cases were more successful with regard to pretrial detainees. *Seale v. Manson, supra* note 20; *Collins v. Schoonfield,* 344 F. Supp. 257 (D. Md. 1972); *Smith v. Sampson,* 349 F. Supp. 268 (D.N.H. 1972). In *Williams. v. Hoyt,* 556 F.2d 1336 (5th Cir. 1977), the court affirmed a trial court determination that a specific sanitation problem justified haircuts of jail inmates. In *Carter v. Noble,* 526 F.2d 677 (5th Cir. 1976), the court approved a jury verdict against a jailer who forcibly cut a jail inmate's hair when the jailer knew that the prisoner was about to be released. *See also Cole v. Flick,* 758 F.2d 124 (3d Cir. 1985)(court adopted the state's argument that long hair may subject prisoners to attacks by "predatory homosexuals").

24. 537 F.2d 214 (5th Cir. 1976). *See also Wilson v. Schillinger,* 761 F.2d 921 (3d Cir. 1985)(Rastafarian not denied equal protection when Native Americans allowed to wear long hair).

25. *Teterud v. Burns,* 522 F.2d 357 (8th Cir. 1975). *See also* the discussion in ch. 5. *Cole v. Flick, supra* note 23 (restrictions on hair length did not violate First Amendment rights of Native American prisoners). *See Wilson v. Schillinger, supra* note 24 (same for Rastafarian); *Shabazz v. Barnauskas,* 600 F. Supp. 712 (M.D. Fla. 1985)(prohibition on beards was not unconstitutional as applied to Muslim inmates).

26. ___ U.S. ___, 107 S. Ct. 2254, ___ L. Ed. 2d___ (1987)(constitutional right to marry includes male inmate marrying female inmate or an inmate marrying a nonprisoner).

27. *Id.* at 2266.

28. *Id.* at 2265 citing *Butler v. Wilson,* 415 U.S. 953, 94 S. Ct. 1479, 39 L. Ed. 2d 569 (1974), summarily affirming *Johnson v. Rockefeller,* 365 F. Supp. 377 (S.D.N.Y. 1973). See also 28 C.F.R. §551.10 (1986)(marriage by federal prisoner generally permitted but not if warden finds that it presents a threat to security or order of institution or to public safety).

29. *Id.* at 2266. The Court stated it need not apply the *Procunier v. Martinez,* 416 U.S. 396, 413-14, 94 S. Ct. 1800, 40 L. Ed. 2d 224

(1974) strict scrutiny standard to the "interests of the non-prisoners. . . . because even under the reasonable relationship test, the marriage regulation does not withstand scrutiny."

30. *Id.* at 2267.

VIII

The Special Concerns of Women Prisoners

One would not think it necessary to include in this book a separate chapter addressing the rights of women in prison. After all, many of the conditions suffered by prisoners exist regardless of sex. Male and female prisoners alike are confined under substandard conditions; they are subject to highly intrusive searches of their persons, possessions, and living areas; they are denied First Amendment rights of speech and free exercise of religion; and they are disciplined and punished without even the rudimentary protections of due process of law.

Nevertheless, a growing body of case law and literature has all too poignantly brought to light that women in prison, more than their male counterparts, are prisoners of their sex with special problems not faced by men in prison. Since women comprise only a small percentage of the prison population, these problems are often overlooked. Yet the problems encountered by women in prisons are peculiarly severe, especially with respect to the inadequate provision of health care services and the inequalities in prison programming.

The problems encountered by women in prison are deserving of separate attention since the legal rights involved are substantially affected by their status as females. This chapter examines some of those problems and, it is hoped, will provide some assistance in the struggle to overcome them.

Are female prisoners entitled to equal treatment in the provision of jobs, vocational, educational, recreational, and other services available to male prisoners?
Yes. At prisons and jails in the United States, women are incarcerated in facilities that separate them from men. Typically, prisons affect this separation through institutions designed exclusively for women. County jails on the other hand, most often segregate women in a unit within the confines of a larger facility. In such segregated prisons and jails the jobs and vocational education programs available to women are vastly inferior to those available to men. Women also have fewer and

less specialized services and facilities. In spite of these differences, the segregation of male and female prisoners, unlike
the segregation of inmates on the basis of race,[1] does not in
and of itself implicate any constitutional or statutory rights.
The segregation of female and male prison populations is generally perceived as a measure in furthering the legitimate security goals of the institution, and no court has ruled that such
a practice is unconstitutional or otherwise unlawful.

Accepting that the confinement of women in separate facilities from men is a necessary incident of imprisonment, prison
litigation on behalf of women inmates has instead focused on
the provision of equal treatment. Courts have been receptive
to claims of female prisoners that their conditions of confinement be at least equal to that of their male counterparts. Thus,
markedly inferior conditions in women's prisons in comparison
to men's prisons have been held to violate the Equal Protection
Clause of the Fourteenth Amendment.[2]

The right to equal treatment is confirmed by this clause. In
order to prevail on an equal protection claim, it is necessary
to establish that the rights claimed by the female prisoners are
among those which have been conferred upon the class of
prisoners as a whole and denied to women because of their
sex. Essentially, the inquiry is one of comparison. Do differences exist in conditions and opportunities offered to the two
populations? Differences do exist. Therefore, courts have not
been reluctant to require correctional administrators to provide
"parity of treatment" to male and female prisoners.[3]

The decision in *Canterino v. Wilson*[4] dramatizes these differences. The court held that officials of the Kentucky Department of Corrections unconstitutionally discriminated against
the inmates at Kentucky's only prison for women. Among the
equal protection violations found were inferior programs, vocational education, training, jobs, and outdoor recreational opportunities when compared to those available to similarly
situated inmates at the state male correctional institutions.

With regard to vocational opportunities and on-the-job training for instance, women prisoners were excluded entirely from
industrial services, agricultural services, and maintenance services. Many of the most valuable and marketable skills such
as plumbing, electrical, masonry, mechanical, and carpentry
could be developed in these services. Instead, most women

were assigned to the chores of cooking and cleaning.[5] The court
had little difficulty in concluding that the disparity in the avail-
abitiy of vocational and training opportunities violated the wom-
en's equal protection rights.[6]

The inequalities in recreational opportunities were even more
dramatic. The court found that the women had virtually no
opportunity to exercise or recreate outdoors since—according
to the prison's superintendent—insufficient staff was available
during the day to safeguard against the possibility of escape.
In contrast, even at the Kentucky male prison which was highly
restricted with regards to yard time, male inmates had the
opportunity to exercise outdoors for at least six hours on a daily
basis.[7] Here again the court had little difficulty concluding that
gender-based discrimination violated the women's equal protection rights.[8]

Another example of the disparity in the provision of services
afforded male and female inmates was at issue in *McMurry v.
Phelps*.[9] There, women felons confined to the parish jail were
prohibited from becoming trusties, from participating in work
release programs, and from transferring to a nearby prison farm.
Similarly situated male inmates could become trusties, and
those at the prison farm had access to contact visitation, work
release programs, drug and alcohol abuse programs, as well as
to outdoor sports and exercise programs, all of which were
denied to women inmates, who were precluded from housing
at the farm.[10] The district court went on to hold the differential
treatment to be unconstitutional sex discrimination.[11]

In *Mitchell v. Untreiner*,[12] the district court similarly found
that women felons confined in a county jail were discriminated
against on the basis of their sex in violation of the Equal Protection Clause. There, only convicted male inmates could become trusties or serve their time in a less severe facility located
nearby. Since only women trusties had the opportunity for
regular exercise, women confined at the jail had virtually no
access to exercise due solely to their sex. Moreover, only inmates incarcerated at the nearby road camp had access to
regular outdoor exercise, contact visits, and educational programs.[13] Since similarly situated women confined at the jail
had no opportunity for contact visits, education, or outdoor
exercise, these women were treated differently from their male
counterparts solely on the basis of their sex.

Finally, in *Glover v. Johnson*,[14] the court recognized the sex-based character of inferior vocational and educational programs offered to women compared to programs available to similarly situated male inmates:

[A] female felon in the State of Michigan will be sent to Huron Valley by reason of her gender alone, and will necessarily have access only to these programs currently available at that location. A male prisoner, on the other hand, can be classified or later transferred to a wide variety of prison facilities in the State and generally will have access to more program opportunities than his female counterpart. I conclude therefore, that because of these limitations women as a group are treated differently than men as a group, and that these differences in treatment are directly related to gender.[15]

The court went on to hold this differential treatment unconstitutional.[16]

Based on the foregoing discussion, the clear answer to the question of whether women prisoners are entitled to equality of treatment in the provision of jobs, education, and other services is an emphatic yes. The Equal Protection Clause of the Fourteenth Amendment has proven to be a powerful ally to protest the lack of a wide range of program services at women's correctional facilities if those same services are available at men's prisons.

What privacy rights do women prisoners have?

To a large extent the privacy rights of women in prison coincide with those available to men prisoners. Thus, like men prisoners, they must surrender many rights of privacy which most people may claim in their private homes. Accordingly, they are subject to highly intrusive searches of their personal possessions and living areas at the discretion of jail administrators.[17] Also like their male counterparts, they may be subjected to strip searches and body cavity searches under appropriate circumstances.[18]

The one area in which most men and women prisoners do retain some degree of privacy is in the performance of such intimate and private affairs as showering, use of the toilet, and otherwise appearing in a state of nudity in the presence of opposite sex correctional officers.

The leading case in this regard is *Forts v. Ward*,[19] a case in which the court recognized that the "privacy interest [of female prisoners who are] entitled to protection concerns the involuntary viewing of private parts of the body by members of the opposite sex."[20] The court thereafter articulated administrative steps which would assure the right of privacy of females in performing certain intimate bodily functions. These included the promulgation of a rule permitting female prisoners to cover the windows of their cell for several minutes at established intervals so as to be able to undress and use the toilet without being subject to staff view and the provision of suitable sleepwear.[21]

The concerns for privacy articulated in *Forts v. Ward* were later relied upon by the Fourth Circuit Court of Appeals in *Lee v. Downs*[22] and *Fisher v. Washington Area Metropolitan Transit Authority*.[23] In *Downs*, the court held that the forced removal of a female inmate's clothing in the presence of a male guard was an unwarranted invasion of privacy. In *Fisher*, the court reached the same conclusion in a case involving the claims of a female arrestee retained naked in a police station isolation cell with an elevated TV camera that relayed a closed-circuit picture to an area where she could be viewed by male policemen.

In sum, while the expectation of privacy in prison is greatly diminished, the courts have shown a special sensitivity to the involuntary exposure of a prisoner's genitals in the presence of people of the opposite sex. The uniform response to the courts has been that when not reasonably necessary, that sort of degradation is not to be visited upon those confined in prisons.

Are women prisoners entitled to adequate health care?

Here again, the rights of female prisoners largely coincide with those of their male counterparts. Thus, although the health care needs of women may differ somewhat from those of men, prison officials must comport with the requirements of the Supreme Court decision in *Estelle v. Gamble*.[24] Under *Gamble*, prison officials are in violation of the Eighth Amendment prescription against unnecessary and wanton infliction of pain when they show a "deliberate indifference" to the serious medical need of prisoners.[25]

The leading case interpreting *Gamble,* one of the few brought by inmates at a woman's correctional facility, is *Todaro v. Ward.*[26] Noting from *Gamble* that inmates are utterly dependent upon the custodians, the *Todaro* court went beyond the *Gamble* standards:

> We have often allowed the recovery of damages when an individual has received improper medical care; *a fortiori* the Constitution does not stand in the way of a broader attack upon the adequacy of an institute's entire health care system which threatens the well-being of many individuals. And while a single instance of medical care denied or delayed, viewed in isolation, may appear to be the product of mere negligence, repeated examples of such treatment bespeak a deliberate indifference by prison authorities to the agony engendered by haphazard and ill-conceived procedures.[27]

The court went on to hold that conditions at New York's Bedford Hills Prison for women constituted cruel and unusual punishment and cited as examples delayed admission screening, a lack of access to primary care physicians, inadequate treatment facilities, and failure to carry out diagnostic work and follow-up care.[28]

The requirements of the Eighth Amendment as interpreted by the *Gamble* and *Todaro* decisions could be used to protect a wide range of deficiencies in women's health care services, including the failure to provide adequate gynecological services and safe abortion and delivery facilities.[29]

Concerning abortion and delivery services, it must be remembered that the Eighth Amendment's proscription against cruel and unusual punishment ensures only that the procedures be performed safely. Thus, although women have a right to have an abortion if they choose,[30] there is no attendant right to have the state pay for it.[31] Although this works a hardship on most prisoners because of their indigency, the courts have not been receptive to their plight.[32] Similarly, it must be understood that while prison authorities must provide safe delivery facilities,[33] they are under no obligation to keep the mother and child together as there is no constitutional or statutory right to raise a child in prison.[34]

NOTES

1. *See* ch. 6.
2. *See, e.g., Canterino v. Wilson,* 546 F. Supp. 174 (W.D. Ky. 1982); *McMurry v. Phelps,* 533 F. Supp. 742 (W.D. La. 1982); *Glover v. Johnson,* 478 F. Supp. 1075 (E.D. Mich. 1979); *Mitchell v. Untreiner,* 421 F. Supp. 886 (N.D. Fla. 1976).
3. *See supra* note 2.
4. *See supra* note 2.
5. *Id.* at 193–94.
6. *Id.* at 212.
7. *Id.* at 201–2.
8. *Id.* at 212.
9. *See supra* note 2.
10. *Id.* at 757–58.
11. *Id.* at 767–68.
12. *See supra* note 2.
13. *Id.* at 892–95.
14. *See supra* note 2.
15. *Id.* at 1078.
16. *Id.* at 1101. Also see, *Dawson v. Kendrick,* 527 F. Supp. 1252 (S.D. W.Va. 1981)(Equal Protection Clause mandates parity in programming); *Buckhari v. Hutto,* 487 F. Supp. 1162 (E.D. Va. 1980)(same); *Inmates of Allegheney County Jail v. Wecht,* 565 F. Supp. 1278 (W.D. Pa. 1983)(equal access to prison law library); *Batton v. State Government of North Carolina,* 501 F. Supp. 1173 (E.D.N.C. 1980)(disparity in prisoner classification system).
17. *Block v. Rutherford,* 468 U.S. 576, 104 S. Ct. 3227, 82 L. Ed. 2d 438 (1984); *Hudson v. Palmer,* 468 U.S. 517, 104 S. Ct. 3194, 82 L. Ed. 2d 393 (1984); *Bell v. Wolfish,* 441 U.S. 520, 99 S. Ct. 1861, 60 L. Ed. 2d 447 (1979). *Also see* discussion in ch. 7.
18. *Bell v. Wolfish, supra* note 17. *Also see* discussion in ch. 7.
19. 621 F.2d 1210 (2d Cir. 1980).
20. *Id.* at 1217.
21. *Id.* at 1216–17. *Also see Dawson v. Kendrick, supra* note 16, at 1316 (same). In the reverse situation, male prisoners are also entitled to judicial protection of the right to privacy deemed by the presence of female guards stationed in positions to observe men while undressed or using toilets. *Cumbey v. Meachum,* 684 F.2d 712 (10th Cir. 1982) and *Bowling v. Enomoto,* 514 F. Supp. 201 (N.D. Cal. 1981).
22. 641 F.2d 1117 (4th Cir. 1981).
23. 690 F.2d 1133 (4th Cir. 1982).

24. 429 U.S. 97, 97 S. Ct. 285, 50 L. Ed. 2d 251 (1976). *Also see* discussion at ch. 8.
25. *Id.* at 104–105.
26. 565 F.2d 48 (2d Cir. 1977).
27. *Id.* at 52.
28. *Id.* at 50–53.
29. *See Newman v. Alabama,* 349 F. Supp. 278 (M.D. Ala. 1972), *modified,* 522 F.2d 71 (5th Cir. 1975), where the court observed that the deplorable conditions in existence at the delivery room in an Alabama prison were such that they imperiled the rights not only of the women prisoners but also of the innocent, noncriminal newborn infants.
30. *Roe v. Wade,* 410 U.S. 113, 93 S. Ct. 705, 35 L. Ed. 2d 147 (1973).
31. *Maher v. Roe,* 432 U.S. 464, 97 S. Ct. 2376, 53 L. Ed. 2d 484 (1977) and *Harris v. McRae,* 448 U.S. 297, 100 S. Ct. 2671, 65 L. Ed. 2d 784 (1980).
32. *But see, Monmouth County Correctional Inst. Inmates v. Lanzaro,* 643 F. Supp. 1217 (D.N.J. 1986), appeal pending, DKT. No. 86-5527 (3d Cir. June 30, 1986)(holding that while pregnant inmates in a county jail have no right to a state financed abortion under United States Constitution, the New Jersey Constitution secures the right).
33. *Newman v. Alabama, supra* note 29.
34. After the prisoner has given birth, the practice of most states is to place the child with the father, relatives, or a welfare agency. Only New York allows the child to remain with the mother for a period of up to one year at the discretion of the prison administration. N.Y. Correct. Law §611(2)(McKinney, 1968). Moreover, the practice of removing newborn infants from the mother has been upheld against constitutional challenge. *Wainwright v. Moore,* 374 So.2d 586 (Fla. Dist. Ct. App. 1979) and *Bailey v. Lombard,* 101 Misc.2d 56, 420 N.Y.S.2d 650 (N.Y. Sup. Ct. 1979). *But see, Apgar v. Beauter,* 75 Misc.2d 439, 347 N.Y.S.2d 872 (N.Y. Sup. Ct. 1973)(state enjoined from taking child of mother awaiting trial).

IX

Medical Care and Rehabilitation

Lack of adequate medical, dental, and psychiatric care is common in most penal institutions. The primary cause of this situation is the lack of competent medical personnel to treat the thousands of men and women who pass through the correctional system each year. In many prisons, only the most serious ailments are treated, and often these are the subject of haphazard and mediocre care; minor ailments are often ignored for lack of a doctor or nurse or for more callous reasons such as the refusal by a guard to allow a prisoner to attend sick call. And even where staff is available, the absence of clear lines of communication and organization between corrections and medical staff results in delays and interference in the provision of medical care. The advent of AIDS in the prison system also raises questions of adequate medical care as well as due process and equal protection issues.

Do prisoners have a right to be provided with medical treatment?
Yes. An increasing number of suits have challenged the quality and nature of medical treatment afforded prisoners. The early attitude of the courts—a manifestation of the "hands-off" policy—was to dismiss all suits which raised questions concerning prison medical practices. Prison officials were deemed the best judges of what treatment was required, and the courts stated that they were not equipped to question these decisions.

That rigid attitude has been relaxed over the past decade.[1] The United States Supreme Court has ruled that the government must provide medical care for those whom it punishes by incarceration. "Deliberate indifference" by prison personnel to an inmate's serious illness or injury constitutes cruel and unusual punishment under the Eighth Amendment.[2] And whether indifference consists of prison doctors in their response to prisoners' needs or guards in denying or delaying access to treatment or interfering with prescribed treatment, the inmates' constitutional rights are violated. Where the mistreatment is inadvertent or the result of negligence, however, no constitutional right is violated, and the prisoner must pursue a malpractice action in state court.

Who decides what treatment a prisoner is entitled to receive?
Prison officials, in practice. The courts have provided little in the way of concrete relief to prisoners because most cases have involved disputes between prisoners and medical officials as to whether medical treatment was sufficient. The courts are most likely to believe the testimony of the doctors and other prison officials that the treatment was adequate. In addition, the courts have held that neither negligence nor a mere difference of opinion between the prisoner and prison officials will support an allegation of inadequate medical care under the Federal Civil Rights Act.

While the prisoner is not, according to the courts, the ultimate judge of what medical treatment is necessary or proper, where he can demonstrate obvious reckless disregard, deliberate indifference,[3] or intentional mistreatment,[4] a remedy will be afforded. Similarly, prison officials may not overrule a doctor's medical judgment concerning a prisoner's treatment.[5] In addition, prisoners have stated viable claims in cases where the treatment provided is "so clearly inadequate as to constitute a refusal of care."[6]

Under these guidelines, courts have found that constitutional rights were denied to individual prisoners in a variety of situations.[7] These include the failure of prison medical authorities to treat a prisoner for previously diagnosed cancer,[8] the refusal of a warden to permit a prisoner to receive medication prescribed by prison doctors,[9] the interference of prison authorities and doctors in the convalescence of a prisoner operated upon by surgeons,[10] the segregation of a prisoner with another known to have tuberculosis,[11] the 22½-hour delay before sending a prisoner to an outside hospital for diagnosis and treatment of a broken arm, even though he had been promptly seen by a nurse and received medication,[12] the denial of a special diabetic diet ordered by a prison doctor,[13] and the treating of an emergency asthmatic attack with inadequate staff and inoperable equipment.[14]

What remedy exists for prisoners who receive negligent or inadequate medical treatment?

Several remedies exist for the individual prisoner where the failure to provide adequate medical care does not rise to constitutional dimensions. Federal prisoners may sue under the Federal Tort Claims Act for money damages for negligent treatment or nontreatment of medical problems, even though such suits may interfere with prison discipline.[15] Similarly, many states have statutes enabling prisoners to sue for medical malpractice or negligence, and state courts have awarded damages to prisoners in cases where their claims would not have been recognized by federal courts.[16] A Louisiana jury awarded $16,000 to a prisoner who received improper, unsupervised treatment for his broken ankle from an inmate medical technician.[17]

Due to recent indications of a more receptive hearing in the courts to medical care claims, some prisoners with serious injuries have obtained sizeable monetary damage awards from settlement of litigation. For example, in 1979 a Virginia prisoner obtained $518,000 from state officials for gross medical maltreatment at the Richmond Penitentiary. In that case, prison officials allowed untrained prisoners to administer overdoses of Prolixin, a major tranquilizer, resulting in the paralysis of both the prisoner's legs and partial paralysis of his arms.[18]

It is also possible to invoke the so-called diversity jurisdiction of the federal courts in order to hear negligence or malpractice claims against prison authorities. Diversity jurisdiction requires that the parties to the lawsuit be citizens of different states and that the amount of damages sued for be above $10,000. In *United States ex rel. Fear v. Rundle*,[19] a Pennsylvania prisoner who was a citizen of Maryland recovered $20,000 in federal court for the mistreatment of a broken wrist.

Can greater change in the way prison health care is delivered be achieved by lawsuits?

Beyond the limited results in the context of individual medical claims, prisoners have won numerous lawsuits in recent years in which particular state prison systems have been found to be totally inadequate and unconstitutional.[20] Relief was granted in these cases in the form of broad injunctive orders requiring prison officials to submit and effectuate detailed plans to provide comprehensive health services and to meet minimum standards for the delivery of health care such as those promulgated by the American Public Health Association and the American Medical Association.[21] Thus, while individual prisoner damage claims have often been dismissed for failure to prove deliberate indifference, class actions seeking injunctive relief have had frequent success where prisoners have alleged and proved a *pattern* of delay, neglect, or incompetence or a "series of incidents closely related in time," evidencing officially sanctioned neglect.[22]

Can prisoners be the subjects of medical experimentation?
In the absence of stringent safeguards, the answer is clearly no. *Kaimowitz v. Dept. of Mental Hygiene*[23] involved an involuntarily detained mental patient upon whom the mental health authorities wished to perform psychosurgery. The court ruled that such a patient could not provide the informed consent required before such an operation could be performed. There have been several other cases in the prison context which have prohibited or limited the forced use of tranquilizers in a behavior modification program or the use of aversive stimuli (e.g., vomit-inducing drugs).[24]

With respect to so-called nontherapeutic experimentation on prisoners, the issues involved here have just begun to reach the courts.[25] Nontherapeutic experimentation refers to studies conducted to obtain information and not to treat any particular individual. Several governmental and other organizations have recognized the problems with such experimentation in the inherently coercive setting of a prison.[26]

Are prisoners entitled to independent diagnostic treatment and care beyond that afforded by prison authorities?
In general, the answer given by the courts is no. Where there is a conflict of opinion between an inmate and the prison medical authorities, it is the opinion of the authorities that will be upheld. However, as the *Tolbert* and *Martinez*[27] cases indicate, there is some movement in this area, especially in the context of conflicts between outside medical specialists and prison doctors. There is also some indication that courts will appoint medical personnel in order to provide an independent assessment of a prisoner's complaint.[28] The major hurdle is the argument made by prison authorities that if such independent examinations and treatment are afforded, then only the more wealthy prisoners will be able to obtain such relief. On the

other hand, if more wealthy prisoners could obtain relief, the Equal Protection Clause may require that similar treatment be afforded to the indigent prisoner.

Do narcotic addicts have a right to treatment in prison?

Several suits have been initiated on behalf of narcotic addicts who suffer withdrawal symptoms, asking the courts to order methadone detoxification programs. The theory of these cases is that narcotic-substitution therapy is the principal medically indicated course of treatment for drug withdrawal and, therefore, prison officials are under a duty to institute this method of treatment for inmates. Courts have held that when current medical practice indicates a particular course of treatment, denial of such treatment constitutes cruel and unusual punishment. Several courts have held that pretrial detainees undergoing a course of treatment for drug addiction involving methadone maintenance prior to their confinement were entitled to continue the treatment in the jail situation.[29]

Methadone detoxification is in increasing use in various prisons. New York City prisons have been using methadone detoxification as a standard practice for several years; the Maryland legislature adopted a measure allowing its use in all state and county jails; and in Philadelphia, in response to a lawsuit, jail officials instituted a methadone detoxification program in its detention facilities.

What medical care are prisoners with AIDS entitled to receive?

The legal standard for medical treatment for prisoners who have AIDS is no different than that for any other medical condition. The problem is that treatment is very expensive, and the disease inevitably results in death. Prison officials may find their budgets threatened and restrict the quality of care for those who are sick. In terms of prisoners' rights—because AIDS is such a new phenomenon—litigation and court decisions are few. Nevertheless, the pace is sure to quicken as the AIDS mortality statistics mount.

Cases have been brought by prisoners with AIDS alleging "deliberate indifference" to a serious medical need. In Arizona, a prisoner with AIDS sued for better care and access to a special diet.[30] The prisoner died before the case was decided, but it has since been converted into a class action seeking the development of a comprehensive correctional policy on care of prisoners with AIDS, ARC, and HIV seropositivity. Another class action in Nevada challenges a broad range of prison conditions, including a complaint of inadequate attention to the medical needs of seropositive prisoners.[31]

Should prisoners be subjected to mandatory AIDS testing?
Only three states have mass screening programs.[32] Most prisons and jails test only for diagnosis, in response to an incident or for blind epidemiological studies.[33] This is consistent with the Centers for Disease Control's recommendation against routine testing of the general population.[34]

Mass screening can be exorbitantly expensive. The test is called Enzyme-Linked ImmunoSorbent Assay (ELISA) and detects only the presence of antibodies to the HIV virus, not the disease itself. A positive test may mean that the individual was infected at some time but does not indicate whether the individual continues to be infected or will become sick with AIDS. In addition, the results are unreliable unless repeated and confirmed with a Western Blot test.[35]

According to a survey conducted jointly by the National Institute of Justice and the American Correctional Association, four jurisdictions account for 70 percent of all prisoner AIDS cases.[36] Thus with the cost, the unreliability of test results, and the disproportionate distribution of rates of infection, mass screening makes little sense.

In addition, mass screening would result in nightmarish problems for prisoners and prison officials. It is very difficult in a prison to maintain confidential medical records. Staff and prisoners are likely to know who is seropositive. Given the degree of hysteria about AIDS coupled with commonly held misinformation about its transmission, a prisoner who is known to be seropositive is likely to experience discrimination and possible violence or other detrimental effects. Finally, mass screening raises the specter of segregation of seropositive prisoners as prison officials are confronted with test results and are pressured to "do something" about the problem. With this array of problems, it's not surprising that current state correctional department policies disfavor mandatory screening.[37] In spite of this, the federal government is considering mass screening of all federal prisoners and is currently conducting a 60-day test of its program to screen everyone upon intake. It also has implemented a program of testing each prisoner thirty days before discharge and reporting the results to chief U.S. probation officers in the district to which the prisoner will be returned.[38]

Many cases have been filed by prisoners who seek mass screening and segregation of seropositive prisoners, alleging that prison officials have not adequately protected them from the risk of infection.[39] These cases reflect the need for education about AIDS in prison. For example, prisoners in a North Carolina case sought mass screening of prisoners and an end to sharing of kitchen facilities, toilets, linen, and clothing with HIV positive prisoners.[40] This and other similar cases have been decided in favor of correctional departments.

Can prisoners with AIDS, ARC, or HIV seropositivity be segregated?

Even though the only medical basis for segregating prisoners with AIDS, ARC, or HIV seropositivity is when the patient's medical condition requires it, segregation is a common—though not a majority—policy at this point.[41] The courts, in cases decided recently, have upheld these policies.

In *Cordero v. Coughlin*,[42] prisoners with AIDS challenged the prison's practice of segregating them from social, recreational, and rehabilitative opportunites in violation of their First, Eighth, and Fourteenth Amendment rights. The court rejected all claims. In its equal protection analysis, it rejected the notion that AIDS victims were a suspect class and found that the state had a legitimate objective in protecting AIDS victims from tensions and harm that could result from other prisoners' fears and that the segregation policy was rationally related to this objective. The Fourteenth Amendment liberty interest claim was denied on the basis of *Hewitt v. Helms*,[43] and the Eighth Amendment claim was rejected because no showing had been made that plaintiffs were denied adequate food, clothing, shelter, sanitation, medical care, and safety. The court also rejected the First Amendment claim on the basis of *Jones v. North Carolina Prisoners Labor Union, Inc.*[44]

In *Powell v. Department of Corrections*,[45] similar issues were raised although the plaintiffs in this case were HIV seropositive, and the court upheld the segregation. These cases suggest that a successful challenge to segregation would have to based solely on an Eighth Amendment claim challenging the conditions of confinement in segregation.

What are the rights of the noninfected to be protected from AIDS or HIV infection?

As noted above, many cases have been filed by prisoners alleging that prison officials have failed to adequately protect them from AIDS while in prison. In most of these cases, prisoners have been unsuccessful in seeking mandatory testing of all prisoners and segregation of those testing positive. In *LaRocca v. Dalsheim,*[46] prisoners argued that the prison administrator had a duty not to allow anyone in or out of prison without screening for AIDS. However, the antibody test was unavailable at the time, and the claim was rejected. The court also noted that should such a test be developed, "its scientific acceptability, coupled with an unreasonable refusal by the State to give it would first have to be established" before it would order screening.[47]

In *Foy v. Owens,*[48] the plaintiff alleged that the high level of rape in his prison made prisoners particularly vulnerable to getting AIDS, but the court held that he had no constitutional claim unless he could state facts about how he was personally at risk for contracting the disease. In *Smith-Bey v. Captain of Guards, Leavenworth,*[49] the court found that prisoners could not complain that prison made them especially vulnerable to the disease because it could only be transmitted sexually or through intravenous drug abuse or tattooing, all of which are impermissible in prison. The court went on to say that it knew of no reason why prisoners should have greater rights than those not in prison.

Do prisoners have a right to education and training?

One of the central vices of prison life is the enforced idleness that inmates must endure. Few prisons provide any meaningful rehabilitation opportunities; in most prisons psychiatric and psychological counseling are nonexistent, and educational programs and vocational training are plainly outdated and inadequate.

The gap between the rhetoric of corrections—rehabilitation, education, training, treatment—and the reality of prison life—idleness, despair, solitude, dehumanization—grows greater each year. The *Manual of Correctional Standards* of the American Correctional Association states that the prison's "basic purpose" is "the rehabilitation of those sent there by society." This sentiment is echoed in state statutes, prison regulations, court decisions, legislative reports, and other official pronouncements, but most prison officials continue to believe that "rehabilitation" is achieved only when the prisoner accepts without question the authoritarian structure and policies of the institution. It should be made clear that we speak of rehabilitation in terms of the opportunity for education and training and not in terms of thought control or institutional conformity.

Despite the rhetoric, no court has directly held that a prisoner is entitled to rehabilitation. Nevertheless, court decisions in clearly analogous areas have laid the groundwork for what may eventually become a successful attack on the lack of rehabilitation services and programs in our prisons. Cases, including those in the Supreme Court involving commitments to mental hospitals,[50] juvenile jails,[51] and other institutions have suggested that officials have a constitutional obligation to provide adequate treatment and/or rehabilitation programs for the inmates of these institutions.

In an increasing number of cases, courts have indicated that the failure of a prison to provide rehabilitative opportunities will be considered in determining whether confinement in the institution amounts to cruel and unusual punishment. The leading case is *Holt v. Sarver*,[52] a class action that sought to upgrade Arkansas prison conditions, in which the court considered the constitutional necessity for rehabilitation in imprisonment of adult criminal offenders. In discussing the need for rehabilitative treatment, the court stated that it was not prepared to constitutionally require rehabilitative attempts as to convicts, but held: "That however, is not quite the end of the matter. The absence of an affirmative program of training and rehabilitation may have constitutional significance where in the absence of such a program conditions and practices exist which militate against reform and rehabilitation."

In the Alabama prison case, the first statewide totality of conditions case, Judge Frank Johnson stated:

An inmate required to live in these circumstances stands no chance of leaving the institution with a more positive and constructive attitude than the one he or she brought in. The evidence reflects that even if rehabilitation programs, adequate in number and quality, were available, whatever benefit might be derived from them could be undone quickly by this inhumane environment. Consequently, this Court finds that these conditions create an environment in which it is impossible for inmates to rehabilitate themselves or to preserve skills and constructive attitudes already possessed even for those who are inclined to do so. Further, this Court finds that these conditions create an environment that not only makes it impossible for inmates to rehabilitate themselves but also makes dehabilitation inevitable.

There can be no question that the present conditions of confinement in the Alabama penal system violate any current judicial definition of cruel and unusual punishment, a situation evidenced by the defendants' admission that serious Eighth Amendment violations exist. In these circumstances, it is the very confinement itself which impermissibly contravenes the Eighth and Fourteenth Amendment rights of the plaintiff class.

The evidence in these cases also establishes that prison conditions are so debilitating that they necessarily deprive inmates of any opportunity to rehabilitate themselves, or even to maintain skills already possessed. While courts have thus far declined to elevate a positive rehabilitation program to the level of a constitutional right, it is clear that a penal system cannot be operated in such a manner that it impedes an inmate's ability to attempt rehabilitation, or simply to avoid physical, mental or social deterioration.[53]

Similarly in Rhode Island, the district court found that the prison conditions as a whole, which included gross idleness, violated the Constitution. "Viewed as part of the debilitating conditions that prevail at Maximum. . . .the near absence of meaningful rehabilitative programs or recreational activity constitutes a failure on defendants' part which rises to constitutional dimensions."[54] The court, as part of the remedy, ordered that the defendants implement a wide variety of meaningful work and educational, recreational, and vocational programs. Similar orders have been issued in Ohio,[55] Oklahoma,[56] and New Mexico.[57] Thus, while courts will not independently consider lack of rehabilitative programs to violate the Eighth Amendment, where the idleness contributes to and causes cruel and unusual punishment courts have been willing to order the provision of meaningful programs for prisoners.[58]

NOTES

1. *See, e.g.,* Alabama—*Newman v. Alabama,* 503 F.2d 1320 (5th Cir. 1974), *cert. denied,* 421 U.S. 948 (1975); Arkansas—*Finney v. Arkansas Bd. of Correction,* 505 F.2d 194 (8th Cir. 1974); Baltimore—*Collins v. Schoonfield,* 363 F. Supp. 1152 (D. Md. 1973); Colorado—*Ramos v. Lamm,* 485 F. Supp. 122 (D. Colo. 1979), *aff'd in relevant part,* 639 F.2d (10th Cir. 1980), *cert. denied,* 101 S. Ct. 1259 (1981); Delaware—*Anderson v. Redman,* 429 F. Supp. 1105 (D. Del. 1977); Florida—*Costello v. Wainwright,* 397 F. Supp. 20 (M.D. Fla. 1975); New York—*Todaro v. Ward,* 431 F. Supp. 1129 (S.D. N.Y. 1977); Oklahoma—*Battle v. Anderson,* 376 F. Supp. 402 (E.D. Okla. 1974); Puerto Rico—*Feliciano v. Barcelo,* 497 F. Supp. 14 (D. P.R. 1979); Rhode Island—*Palmigiano v. Garrahy,* 443 F. Supp. 956 (D. R.I. 1977); Texas—*Ruiz v. Estelle,* 503 F. Supp. 1265 (S.D. Tex. 1980), *aff'd in relevant part,* 679 F.2d 1115 (5th Cir. 1982); Vermont—*Bishop v. Stoneman,* 508 F.2d 1224 (2d Cir. 1974); Virgin Islands—*Barnes v. Virgin Islands,* 415 F. Supp. 1218 (D.V.I. 1976).
2. *Estelle v. Gamble,* 429 U.S. 97, 97 S. Ct. 285, 50 L. Ed. 2d 251 (1976). *Also see City of Revere v. Massachusetts General Hospital,* 463 U.S. 239, 103 S. Ct. 2979, 77 L. Ed. 2d 605 (1983).
3. *Estelle v. Gamble, supra* note 2; *Benson v. Cady,* 761 F.2d 335, 339 (7th Cir. 1985); *Cody v. Hillard,* 599 F. Supp. 1025 (D.S.D. 1984).
4. *Talley v. Stephens,* 247 F. Supp. 683 (E.D. Ark. 1965).
5. *Martinez v. Mancusi,* 443 F.2d 421 (2d Cir. 1970) and *Tolbert v. Eyman,* 434 F.2d 625 (9th Cir. 1970).
6. *Green v. Carlson,* 581 F.2d 669 (7th Cir. 1978), *aff'd sub nom. Carlson v. Green,* 446 U.S. 14, 100 S. Ct. 1468, 64 L. Ed. 2d 15 (1980).
7. *See* Neisser, "Is There a Doctor in the Joint? The Search for Constitutional Standards for Prison Health Care." 63 Va. L. Rev. 921 (1977).
8. *Sawyer v. Sigler,* 320 F. Supp. 690 (D. Neb. 1970). *Cf. McCarthy v. Weinberg,* 753 F.2d 836 (10th Cir. 1985) (plaintiff suffering from multiple sclerosis denied physical therapy and medication).

9. *Tolbert v. Eyman, supra* note 5. *Also see Ronson v. New* York, 106 F.R.D. 253 (S.D.N.Y. 1985).

10. *Martinez v. Mancusi, supra* note 5. *Also see Shapley v. Nevada Bd. of State Prison Comm'rs.*, 766 F.2d 404, 408 (9th Cir. 1985).

11. *Freeman v. Lockhart*, 503 F.2d 1016 (8th Cir. 1974).

12. *Loe v. Armistead*, 582 F.2d 1291 (4th Cir. 1978).

13. *Johnson v. Harris*, 479 F. Supp. 333 (S.D.N.Y. 1979).

14. *Green v. Carlson, supra* note 6. *Also see* jail medical cases in ch. 10.

15. *United States v. Muniz*, 374 U.S. 150, 83 S. Ct. 1850, 10 L. Ed. 2d 805 (1963). *Also see Green v. Carlson, supra* note 6, 446 U.S. at 19–20.

16. *E.g.*, New York and California.

17. *Dancer v. Dept. of Corrections*, 282 So.2d 730 (La. 1973).

18. *Tucker v. Hutto*, Civ. Act. No. 78-0161 R (E.D. Va. 1979).

19. 364 F. Supp. 53 (E.D. Pa. 1973), *aff'd* 506 F.2d 331 (3d Cir. 1974), *cert. denied sub nom. Anderson v. Fear*, 421 U.S. 1012 (1975).

20. *French v. Owens*, 777 F.2d 1250 (7th Cir. 1985); *Wellman v. Faulkner*, 715 F.2d 269 (7th Cir. 1983); *Ramos v. Lamm*, 485 F. Supp. 122 (D. Cal. 1979), *aff'd in pertinent part*, 639 F.2d 559 (10th Cir. 1980), *cert. denied* 101 S. Ct. 1259 (1981); *Smith v. Sullivan*, 611 F.2d 1039 (5th Cir. 1980); *Todaro v. Ward*, 565 F.2d 48 (2d Cir. 1977); *Miller v. Carson*, 401 F. Supp. 835 (M.D. Fla. 1975), *aff'd in part, mod. in part and remanded*, 563 F.2d 741 (5th Cir. 1977); *Bishop v. Stoneman*, 508 F.2d 1224 (1st Cir. 1974); *Finney v. Arkansas Bd. of Corrections*, 505 F.2d 194 (5th Cir. 1974); *Newman v. State*, 349 F. Supp. 278 (M.D. Ala. 1972), *aff'd* 503 F.2d 1320 (5th Cir. 1974), *cert. denied* 421 U.S. 948 (1975); *Gates v. Collier*, 349 F. Supp. 881 (N.D. Miss. 1972), *aff'd* 501 F.2d 1291 (5th Cir. 1974); *Jones v. Wittenberg*, 330 F. Supp. 707 (N.D. Ohio 1971), *aff'd sub nom. Jones v. Metzger*, 456 F.2d 854 (6th Cir. 1972); *Cody v. Hillard*, 599 F. Supp. 1025 (D. S.D. 1984); *Grubbs v. Bradley*, 552 F. Supp. 1052 (M.D. Tenn. 1982); *Lightfoot v. Walker*, 486 F. Supp. 504 (S.D. Ill. 1980); *Palmigiano v. Garrahy*, 443 F. Supp. 956 (D.R.I. 1977); *Morgan v. Sproat*, 432 F. Supp. 1130 (S.D. Miss. 1977); *Mitchell v. Untreiner*, 421 F. Supp. 886 (N.D. Fla. 1976); *Battle v. Anderson*, 376 F. Supp. 402 (E.D. Okla. 1974). *Also see* Winner, "An Introduction to the Constitutional Law of Prison Medical Care," *Journal of Prison Health* 67 (1981).

21. Besides the cases cited in note 20, *supra*, *see also Goldsby v. Carnes*, 365 F. Supp. 395 (W.D. Mo. 1973) (consent judgment embodying detailed plan for delivery of health care and services).

22. *Todaro v. Ward, supra* note 20. *Also see Benson v. Cady, supra* note 3.

23. 2 Prison L.Rptr. 433 (Cir. Ct. Wayne Co., Mich. 1973).

24. *Mackey v. Procunier*, 477 F.2d 877 (9th Cir. 1973); *Nelson v. Heyne*, 491 F.2d 352 (7th Cir. 1974), *cert. denied* 417 U.S. 976 (1979); *Souder v. McGuire*, 423 F. Supp. 830 (M.D. Pa. 1976); *Clay v. Martin*, 509 F.2d 109 (2d Cir. 1975); *Pena. v. N.Y.S. Div. for Youth*, 419 F. Supp. 203 (S.D.N.Y. 1976); *Scott v. Plante*, 532 F.2d 939 (3d Cir. 1976); and *Martarella v. Kelley*, 349 F. Supp. 575 (S.D.N.Y. 1972).

25. In *Bailey v. Mandel*, 481 F. Supp. 203 (D. Md. 1979), prisoners were denied damages for medical experimentation conducted in Maryland prisons from 1958–1976 because the law was not clearly established at that time prohibiting such conduct and because coercion was not demonstrated by plaintiffs.

26. *See* discussion in the South Carolina Dept. of Corrections', *The Emerging Rights of the Confined* (1972) 155 and "Guidelines of the National Institutes of Health for the Protection of Human Subjects in Medical Experiments," 39 Fed. Reg. 194, Oct. 9, 1973, and 38 Fed. Reg. 221, Nov. 16, 1973. These guidelines were adopted as 45 C.F.R. Pt. 46 (1975 Supp.). In 1974, Congress adopted the National Research Act and created a National Commission for the Protection of Human Subjects of Biomedical and Behavioral Research, Pub. L. No. 93-348; 88 Stat. 42; 42 U.S.C. § 218, *et seq.*

27. *See supra* note 5.

28. *Lopez Tijerina v. Ciccone*, 324 F. Supp. 1265 (W.D. Mo. 1971). Also see *Prushinowski v. Hambrick*, 570 F. Supp. 863 (E.D.N.C. 1983) (medical furlough ordered so that prisoner could obtain outside doctor's opinion).

29. *See, e.g., Cudnik v. Kreiger*, 392 F. Supp. 305 (N.D. Ohio 1974). *Also see* discussion in ch. 10.

30. *Brown v. Arizona Dep't. of Corrections*, C.A. No. Civ-85-2709-PHX-PGR (MM)(D. Ariz. filed 1986).

31. *Burns v. State of Nevada*, No. CV-S-86-366-HDM (U.S.D.C. Nev.).

32. Hammett, Theodore M., "National Institute of Justice Update: Issues and Practices, AIDS in Correctional Facilities." U.S. Dep't. of Justice, Jan. 1987, at 16. [Hereinafter "NIJ Update"].

33. *Id.*

34. Centers for Disease Control, "Recommended Additional Guidelines for HIV Antibody Counseling and Testing in the Prevention of HIV Infection and AIDS." U.S. Department of Health and Human Services, Apr. 30, 1987.

35. Robert Cohen, "Medical Expert Views Potential for Abuse in AIDS Screening," *National Prison Project Journal*, Winter 1985.

36. New York State, New York City, New Jersey, and Florida. *See*, "NIJ Update," at 16.

37. The National Ass'n. of State Corrections Administrators voted against mandatory testing in Jan., 1986. See also "NIJ Update," at 16.

38. Federal Bureau of Prisons, Operation Memorandum No. 73–87 (6100), June 24, 1987, "Human Immuno-Deficiency Virus Admission and Pre-Release Program". Available from Federal Bureau of Prisons, General Counsels' Office, HOLC Building, 320 First Street, N.W., Washington, D.C. 20534.

39. *Mayberry v. Martin*, C.A. No. 86-341-CRT (E.D.N.C. decision pending); *Herring v. Keeney*, C.A. No. __ (D. Or. filed Sept. 17, 1985), *Sheppard v. Keeney*, C.A. No. __ (D. Or. filed Oct. 7, 1985), *Mapport v. Keeney*, C.A. No. __ (D. Or. filed Oct. 11, 1985) (these three cases seek mass HIV testing; *Hook v. Fauver*, C.A. No. 85-5962 (HAA) (D.N.J. 1985) (a pending case seeks better screening and education procedures, seeks segregation of high risk and symptomatic inmates); *Potter v. Wainwright*, C.A. No. 85-1616-CIV-T15 (M.D. Fla. 1985) (pending case seeks mandatory HIV testing); *Knight v. Henderson*, C.A. No. PB-C-86-16 (D. Ark. 1986) (pending case seeks mass screening, hospitalization of PWAs, discharge of staff with AIDS, removal of seropositive staff from contact with inmates and staff, and reporting of names of people with AIDS); *Yates v. Lewis*, C.A. No. CIV-86-1538-PHX (D. Ariz. 1986) (pending case seeks damages for severe emotional distress for being housed in same unit as prisoners with ARC).

40. *Wiedman v. Rogers*, C.A. No. C-85-116-6 (E.D.N.C. filed 1986).

41. "NIJ Update," at 20–21. The trend, however, is away from segregation of prisoners with ARC and HIV seropositivity.

42. 607 F. Supp. 9 (S.D.N.Y. 1984).

43. 655 F.2d 487 (3d Cir. 1981), *rev'd* 459 U.S. 460, 103 S. Ct. 864, 74 L. Ed. 2d 675 (1983), *on remand* 712 F.2d 48 (3d Cir. 1983).

44. 409 F. Supp. 937 (N.D.N.C. 1976), *rev'd* 433 U.S. 119, 97 S. Ct. 2532, 53 L. Ed. 2d 629 (1977).

45. C.A. Nos. 85-C-820-C and 85-C-816-B (N.D. Okla. Feb. 20, 1986).

46. 120 Misc. 2d. 697, (N.Y. 1983).

47. *Id.* at 700.

48. C.A. No. 85-6909 (E.D. Pa. Mar. 19, 1986).

49. C.A. No. 86-3274 (D. Kan. Dec. 11, 1986).

50. *Rouse v. Cameron*, 373 F.2d 451 (D.C. Cir. 1966); *Jackson v. Indiana*, 406 U.S. 715, 92 S. Ct. 1845, 32 L. Ed. 2d 435 (1972); *Wyatt v. Stickney*, 344 F. Supp. 373 (M.D. Ala. 1972), *modified sub nom. Wyatt v. Aderholt*, 503 F.2d 1305 (5th Cir. 1974).

51. *Creek v. Stone*, 379 F.2d 106 (D.C. Cir. 1967); *Nelson v. Heyne*, 491 F.2d 352 (7th Cir. 1974); *Morales v. Turman*, 383 F. Supp. 53 and

364 F. Supp. 166 (E.D. Tex. 1973); *Martarella v. Kelly,* 349 F. Supp. 575 (S.D.N.Y. 1972) and 359 F. Supp. 478 (S.D.N.Y. 1973).

52. 309 F. Supp. 362 (E.D. Ark. 1970), *aff'd* 442 F.2d 304 (8th Cir. 1971).

53. *Pugh v. Locke,* 406 F. Supp. 318 (M.D. Ala. 1976) *aff'd sub nom. Newman v. Alabama,* 559 F.2d 283 (5th Cir. 1977), *cert.denied in pertinent part,* 438 U.S. 78 (1978).

54. *Palmigiano v. Garrahy, supra* note 1, at 981.

55. *Jones v. Wittenberg, supra* note 20.

56. *Battle v. Anderson,* 376 F. Supp. 402 (E.D. Okla. 1974), subseq. unpub. opinion, *aff'd* 564 F.2d 388 (10th Cir. 1977).

57. *Duran v. Apodoca,* Cir. 77-721C (D.N.M. 1980)(consent decree).

58. *See Rhodes v. Chapman* 452 U.S. 337, 369, 101 S. Ct. 2392, 69 L. Ed. 2d 59 (1981) (Brennan, J. concurring).

X

Pretrial Confinement:
Jail Conditions and Practices

However desperate the conditions in many state prisons, they are far better than those that prevail in the thousands of jails around the country used to detain persons awaiting trial and to imprison convicts serving short prison sentences. The jails are an unmitigated disgrace. They are overcrowded, understaffed, unsanitary, and structurally deteriorating. They give little protection from physical and sexual assaults, provide virtually no programs, and spend almost their entire budgets on security. In short, they exist only to warehouse those persons charged with a crime who are too poor to post bail for their release.

Moreover, the recent surge in jail population[1]—due to more aggressive law enforcement tactics, defense delaying tactics, and harsher sentencing and parole policies—has meant further crowding of these locally supported facilities. The crowding, the failure to construct facilities to keep pace with the influx, and the reluctance to implement alternative and diversional programs has meant further deterioration of conditions, services, and supervision. Sheriffs and jail staff have become alarmed as control is lost.

Detainees encounter many of the same legal problems as prisoners in state prisons. They too are subject to substandard physical conditions; they are denied First Amendment rights of communication; and they are disciplined and punished without even the rudimentary protections of due process of law.

But jails deserve separate attention since the legal rights involved are affected substantially by the fact that jail inmates are for the most part awaiting trial on criminal charges and therefore, under the law, are presumed innocent. Theoretically at least, and under Supreme Court decisions, detention is for the sole purpose of ensuring a defendant's appearance at trial and is not for punishment.[2] In practice, however, sentenced prisoners are usually provided with better conditions than detainees who can expect to have their physical living conditions improve immediately upon sentencing and transfer to a state prison.

Jail conditions deserve special attention, also, considering the number of persons who enter them each year. Over eight million people went through these facilities in the year ending 30 June 1983, the latest statistics on this subject.[3] Public drunks, addicts, the mentally ill, juveniles, minor and major criminals, parents who fail to pay child support, and drunk drivers at one time or another find themselves confined in jails. In many ways, the local jail is the repository for the entire range of social and community ills. Municipalities and other local governments who are responsible for maintaining these facilities must struggle to provide even minimum resources to carry out their obligations imposed by law. Very often they fail.

Of immediate concern to detainees are two problems—the reduction of bail to a reasonable level (and acquiring even that amount) and the proper preparation of the case. Much has been written on these topics, and repetition here would serve no purpose. Suffice it to say that the money bail system as presently constituted is the most irrational and oppressive aspect of our entire system of criminal justice. It puts a price tag on liberty and serves to preventively detain only the poor. The recent action by the Supreme Court in upholding the federal preventive detention law permitting persons to be held without bail on the basis of their predicted future conduct will provide a basis for the passage of similar state laws.[4]

What are the legal rights of pretrial detainees?

A 1979 decision of the United States Supreme Court has established that pretrial detainees can invoke the protections of the Fourteenth Amendment Due Process Clause to force jail administrators to improve poor physical conditions, provide adequate physical protection, and modify or prohibit arbitrary jail rules and practices. The proper analysis, according to the Court in *Bell v. Wolfish*,[5] is to determine if detainees are subjected to punishment. If a challenged condition or restriction is so arbitrary or purposeless (not reasonably related to one of the legitimate governmental goals of institutional security, order, or discipline), then it can be considered punitive. The Court, in establishing this "rational basis" standard, rejected the much more stringent "compelling necessity test" established in pre-1979 appellate cases. Moreover, the case established the principle that courts should "defer to expert judgment [of jail officials] in matters related to security unless there is 'substantial evidence in the record that officials have exaggerated their response to these conditions.' "[6]

Although, in general, this case can be viewed as a backward step for the rights of detainees, the lower federal courts (as well as some state courts) have continued to entertain lawsuits which challenge harsh conditions of confinement and to enter and enforce orders designed to obtain relief for detainees. Many of these orders have been sustained on appeal. It should be emphasized that the jail which was the subject of *Bell v. Wolfish* was the Federal Metropolitan Correction Center in New York City, described by the Court as having "the most advanced and innovative features of modern design of detention facilities." This is a far cry from the horrendous conditions of confinement found presently in the typical American city or county jail.

A recent decision from a Georgia district court enforcing a previous order in the case is illustrative. After firsthand observation of the conditions at the Chatham County Jail, the court said:

> I will not attempt here to detail again the extraordinary abundance of intolerable conditions which citizens have been forced to endure, often as pretrial detainees who have been convicted of no wrongdoing and thus merit no punishment whatever, much less the horrendous combination of fear, filth and neglect in which they now exist.[7]

The court required that the jail's population be reduced by steps, including a transfer of sentenced prisoners into the state system and the expedited trial of detainees. Sanitation at the jail was ordered improved as well as the delivery of medical and dental services. The district judge rejected the argument that political disputes between the commissioners and the sheriff are a defense to compliance with the court's orders.[8] The court identified the lack of a full-time professional administrator as a major problem and ordered that the defendants rectify this situation immediately.[9]

The time for patience is at an end. . . . Should it be shown that the County Commissioners have failed to provide adequate resources to permit these fundamental requirements, the Court will. . . .be compelled to act. . . .I have no wish to remove this public facility from the control of representatives of the taxpayers who must in any event support it. . . .Nonetheless, the Court has its own duty to the citizens of this community, including those who find themselves incarcerated. That duty will be fulfilled.[10]

Similarly, other courts have reviewed jail conditions after the *Wolfish* decision and, finding them wanting, have ordered relief.[11] On the other hand, some courts, after applying *Wolfish*, have found particular conditions in those facilities meet constitutional requirements.[12]

Pre-*Wolfish* cases, although they no longer represent the prevailing law in the area, produced judicial orders calling for positive improvements, many of which are still in effect. Jail facilities were strongly condemned in Philadelphia; Detroit; New Orleans; Toledo; Oakland; Baltimore; St. Louis; Boston; Jacksonville, Florida; and Houston,[13] as well as in many other localities across the country.

Do detainees have other rights besides those stemming from the Due Process Clause of the Constitution?

Yes. *Bell v. Wolfish* indicates in a number of places that detainees, independent of their rights under the Due Process Clause, are entitled to the protections of other provisions of the Constitution.[14] However, the decision has cast doubt on the extent to which detainees can invoke these other basic legal guarantees and challenge jail regulation and practices. For example, in the later portion of its opinion, the Court decided that "the publishers-only rule" did not violate the rights of detainees. The publishers-only rule at issue in *Wolfish* permitted hardcover publications to be received by detainees but only if sent directly from publishers and bookstores. (Soft-covered publications can be received from any source, including family and friends.) The Court's decision noted that the rule "operated in a neutral fashion, without regard to the content of the expression"; there were alternative means of obtaining the publications; and the rule operated in a facility that confined prisoners for only sixty days.[15]

Bell v. Wolfish also limited detainee rights under the Fourth Amendment by upholding jail practices and rules permitting cell searches without the presence of the detainee whose cell is searched and body cavity searches after every contact visit with a person from outside the institution.[16]

The lower federal courts have, in the wake of *Wolfish*, attempted to narrow the reach of the ruling, particularly with respect to this "deference" principle by continuing to scrutinize carefully the security defenses raised by jail officials. One district court has observed that *Wolfish* requires deference, not abdication, of judicial responsibilities;[17] while a court of appeals declared, "We do not read anything in *Wolfish* as requiring this court to grant automatic deference to ritual incantations by prison officials that their actions foster the goals of order and discipline."[18]

Do pretrial detainees have a right to contact visits with family and friends?

No. The Supreme Court has ruled that the Constitution does not require that jail authorities permit contact (or nonbarrier) visits between detainees and their family and friends. In *Block v. Rutherford*,[19] the Court held that a rule prohibiting such visits is a reasonable, nonpunitive response to legitimate security concerns. However, state courts interpreting state law provisions have held that contact visitation is required.[20]

Do pretrial detainees have more rights than sentenced prisoners?

Yes, however the extent of the enhanced rights held by detainees is yet to be determined. According to *Bell v. Wolfish*, pretrial detainees may not be punished,[21] and any punishment meted out would violate the Due Process Clause of the Fourteenth Amendment. It stands to reason (and the courts have so held) that any violation of the ban on cruel and unusual punishment (under the Fourth Amendment) necessarily violates the Due Process Clause as well. "[T]he due process rights of a [pretrial detainee] are *at least as great* as the Eighth Amendment protections available to a convicted prisoner."[22] The plain implication of this language is that pretrial detainees possess a level of rights over and above those held by convicted prisoners. In practical terms, however, the limits of this analysis—except for medical care (see below)—is an issue that will necessarily be explained in future cases.

What are detainees' rights to medical care and treatment?
The answer to this question seems to be that detainees have the same rights as sentenced prisoners. For an analysis of those rights, see chapter 9. The post-*Wolfish* cases in the main rely upon the cases taken from the prison context. In *Inmates of Allegheny County Jail v. Pierce*, for example, the court held that detainees at a minimum are entitled to necessary psychological and psychiatric treatment for serious mental and emotional problems.[23] The district court, in *LaReau v. Manson*, ordered that the authorities "conduct medical examinations and tests which identify these newly-admitted [jail] inmates who may have a communicable disease and. . . .isolate such inmates from other inmates." This order was made more specific in the Court of Appeals.[24]

In the medical context, damages have been awarded to detainees for violation of their rights to obtain needed medical or psychiatric care. A jury in *Reeves v. City of Jackson*[25] held jail officials liable for damages to an arrestee confined to a jail's drunk tank when he died as a result of a stroke. The officials knew or should have known that he was ill rather than drunk when he failed to "sober up" after ten hours.[26]

In *Littlefield v. Deland*,[27] the court of appeals upheld the district court finding that the county was liable for subjecting a mentally ill detainee to terrible conditions in an isolation cell and for failing to provide appropriate treatment for his illness. A jail prisoner held in the segregation unit was denied his right to see a doctor as well as his medication for his skin condition, despite his repeated requests. The prisoner's lawsuit for damages, *Mathis v. DiGiacinto*,[28] was held actionable.

Pretrial detainees may have greater rights than convicted prisoners based on their legal status.[29] The precise limits of these enhanced rights are yet to be worked out. However, some recent developments in the area of medical care suggest that the courts will require a lesser standard when reviewing medical claims presented by pretrial prisoners than when reviewing such claims brought by convicted prisoners.[30] These cases hold that detainees need not allege or prove that the officials deliberately disregarded or were deliberately indifferent to the detainees' serious medical needs in order to prevail. However, the courts have failed to set out what the appropriate, less-restrictive standard might indeed be.

What are detainees' rights to counsel and to legal assistance?
The need to maintain contact with lawyers who are preparing their defense to criminal charges is of major importance to detainees.

According to the judicial decisions on this point, access to counsel also includes availability of facilities for confidential interviews, correspondence, and telephone calls. Where there are no reasonable alternatives, jail authorities must permit other prisoners (called "jailhouse lawyers") to provide legal assistance. The law also requires the establishment and maintenance of systems for reasonable access to law library facilities as well as requiring jail authorities to allow access to the facilities.[31]

NOTES

1. Statistics for 1978 confirm that 158,394 persons were confined to jails; that number increased to 223,551 in 1983. This represents a 41 percent increase in the period. Bureau of Justice Statistics, U.S. Dep't. of Justice, "The 1983 Jail Census," *Bulletin*, (Nov. 1984), Table 2.
2. *Ingraham v. Wright*, 430 U.S. 651, 671–72, n.40, 97 S. Ct. 1401, 51 L. Ed. 2d 711 (1977) and *Bell v. Wolfish*, 441 U.S. 520, 535, 99 S. Ct. 1861, 60 L. Ed. 2d 447 (1979).
3. Bureau of Justice Statistics, U.S. Dep't. of Justice, "The 1983 Jail Census," *Bulletin*, (Nov. 1984), at 4, Table 7.
4. *U.S. v. Salerno*, __U.S.__, 107 S. Ct. 2095, __L. Ed. 2d__ (1987).
5. *See* note 2, supra.
6. *Id.* at 548.
7. *Mercer v. Griffin*, 30 Cr.L. 2253, No. CV 474-195 (S.D. Ga. Nov. 20, 1981).
8. *Id.* at 5.
9. *Id.* at 6–7.
10. *Id.* at 9–10.
11. *Malone v. Colyer*, 710 F.2d 258 (6th Cir. 1983); *LaReau v. Manson*, 507 F. Supp. 1177 (D. Conn. 1980), *aff'd in part and modified in part*, 651 F.2d 96 (2d Cir. 1981); *Lock v. Jenkins*, 641 F.2d 488 (7th Cir. 1981); *Jones v. Diamond*, 636 F.2d 1364 (5th Cir. 1981)(*en banc*), *cert. dismissed sub nom. Ledbetter v. Jones*, 453 U.S. 950 (1981);

Leeds v. Watson, 630 F.2d 674 (9th Cir. 1980); Campbell v. Cauthron, 623 F.2d 503 (8th Cir. 1980); Heitman v. Gabriel, 524 F. Supp. 622 (W.D. Mo. 1981); Monmouth County Correctional Inst. Inmates v. Lanzaro, 595 F. Supp. 1417 (D.N.J. 1984); Inmates of Allegheny County Jail v. Wecht, 565 F. Supp. 1278 (W.D. Pa. 1983); Fischer v. Winter, 564 F. Supp. 281 (N.D. Cal. 1983); Martino v. Carey, 563 F. Supp. 984 (D. Or. 1983); Hutchings v. Corum, 501 F. Supp. 1276 (W.D. Mo. 1980); Palmigiano v. Garrahy, 639 F. Supp. 244 (D.R.I. 1986); Reece v. Gragg, 650 F. Supp. 1297, No. 82-1970 (D.Kan. Dec. 17, 1986); Powlowski v. Wullich, 102 A.D.2d 575 (N.Y. App. Div. 4th Dept. 1984); In re Inmates of Riverside County Jail at Indo v. Clark, 144 Cal.3rd 850, 192 Cal. Rptr. 823 (Cal. Ct. App. 4th Dist. 1983); Morales v. County of Hudson, No. C-2602-80 (N.J. Chan. Div. Hudson Co., Superior Ct. May 19, 1982); Wickham v. Fisher, 629 P.2d 896 (Utah S. Ct. 1981).

12. *Union County Jail Inmates v. DiBuono*, 713 F.2d 984 (3d Cir. 1983), *rehearing denied*, 718 F.2d 1247 (3d Cir. 1983)(Gibbons, J., dissenting); *Jordan v. Wolke*, 615 F.2d 749, 754 (7th Cir. 1980)(Swygert, J., dissenting); *Bradford v. Gardner*, 578 F. Supp. 382 (E.D. Tenn. 1984).

13. *Commonwealth ex rel. Bryant v. Hendrick*, 444 Pa. 83, 280 A.2d 110 (Pa. 1971), *on remand Jackson v. Hendrick*, 11 Cr. L. 2088 (Phil. Ct. Comm. Pleas Apr. 7, 1972), *aff'd* 457 Pa. 405, 321 A.2d 603 (Pa. S. Ct. 1974), *on remand* __Pa.__, 1 PLM 57 (Phila. Ct. Comm. Pleas Dec. 1, 1977)(contempt finding); *Wayne County Jail Inmates v. Lucas*, No. 173217 (Wayne Co. Cir. Ct. 1971), *aff'd*, 391 Mich. 359, 216 N.W.2d 910, (Mich. 1974); *Hamilton v. Love*, 328 F. Supp. 1182 (E.D. Ark. 1971); *Jones v. Wittenberg*, 323 F. Supp. 93 (N.D. Ohio 1971), *aff'd* 456 F.2d 854 (6th Cir. 1972); *Brenneman v. Madigan*, 343 F. Supp. 128 (N.D. Cal. 1972); *Collins v. Schoonfield*, 344 F. Supp. 257 (D. Md. 1972); *Johnson v. Lark*, 365 F. Supp. 289 (E.D. Mo. 1973); *Inmates of Suffolk County Jail v. Eisenstadt*, 360 F. Supp. 676 (D. Mass. 1973), *aff'd* 518 F.2d 1241 (1st Cir. 1975); *Miller v. Carson*, 401 F. Supp. 835 (M.D. Fla. 1975), *aff'd in part and modified in part* 563 F.2d 741 (5th Cir. 1977); *Alberti v. Sheriff*, 406 F. Supp. 649 (S.D. Tex. 1975).

14. 441 U.S. at 535, 537–38, 551–52 and 559.

15. *Id.* at 552–53.

16. *Id.* at 556–58. *See also Block v. Rutherford*, 468 U.S. 576, 104 S. Ct. 3227, 82 L. Ed. 2d 438 (1984)(ban on contact visiting not unconstitutional).

17. *Beckett v. Powers*, 494 F. Supp. 364 (W.D. Wis. 1980).

18. *Lock v. Jenkins, supra* note 10 at 498.

19. *See supra* note 16.

20. *Cooper v. Morin,* 49 N.Y.2d 69, 399 N.E.2d 1188 (N.Y. 1979); and
    Wickham v. Fisher, supra note 10 (contact visits can occur "if
    practicable").
21. 441 U.S. at 545.
22. *City of Revere v. Massachusetts General Hospital,* 463 U.S. 239, 244,
    103 S. Ct. 2979, 77 L. Ed. 2d (1983)(emphasis added).
23. 612 F.2d 754, 763 (3d Cir. 1979).
24. 507 F. Supp. at 1194, 651 F.2d at 109. *See also Heitman v. Gabriel,*
    524 F. Supp. at 627–28.
25. 608 F.2d 644 (5th Cir. 1979).
26. *See also Anderson v. City of Atlanta,* 778 F.2d 678 (11th Cir. 1985);
    Garcia v. Salt Lake County, 768 F.2d 303 (10th Cir. 1985); *Aldridge
    v. Montgomery,* 753 F.2d 970 (11th Cir. 1985); *Goodman v. Wagner,*
    553 F. Supp. 255 (E.D. Pa. 1982).
27. *Littlefield v. Deland,* 641 F.2d 729 (10th Cir. 1981).
28. 430 F. Supp. 457 (E.D. Pa. 1977).
29. *Aldridge v. Montgomery, supra* note 26, at 972; *Matzker v. Herr,* 748
    F.2d 1142 (7th Cir. 1984); *Whisenant v. Yuam,* 739 F.2d 160 (4th Cir.
    1984); *Kincaid v. Rusk,* 670 F.2d 737, 743 n.8 (7th Cir. 1982). *See
    also Bell v. Wolfish, supra* note 2, at 545.
30. *See supra* note 29.
31. *See* ch. 3. *Also see* with respect to jails: *Green v. Ferrell,* 801 F.2d
    765 (5th Cir. 1986)(jail legal assistance program found inadequate
    where prisoners permitted to request two volumes at a time from
    inventory lists; lawyer representation on criminal case insufficient to
    defeat claim); *Carter v. Fair,* 786 F.2d 433 (1st Cir. 1986)(jail legal
    assistance program found adequate where lawyer available for more
    than three hours per week and provide advice but not extensive outside
    research); *Morrow v. Harwell,* 768 F.2d 619 (5th Cir. 1985)(adequate
    access to legal assistance not provided by weekly visits of county library
    bookmobile nor by circumscribed assistance of two law students); *Leeds
    v. Watson,* 630 F.2d 674 (9th Cir. 1980)(availability of county law
    library with court order inadequate); *Cruz v. Hauk,* 627 F.2d 710 (5th
    Cir. 1980)(suggests hours of availability of jail law library should be
    extended; that presence of trained librarian or paralegal may be re-
    quired; and that even if a library was provided, other legal assistance
    might be required); *Cobb v. Aytch,* 643 F.2d 946 (3d Cir. 1981)(rights
    of pretrial prisoners to remain near criminal defense counsel); *Johnson
    v. Galli,* 596 F. Supp. 135 (D. Nev. 1984)(reasonable access to jail
    law library includes right to browse); and *Sykes v. Kreiger,* 451 F.
    Supp. 421 (N.D. Ohio 1975)(right of access to attorneys, students, or
    other agents of lawyers). Confidential correspondence: *Taylor v. Ster-
    rett,* 532 F.2d 462 (5th Cir. 1976); *Dawson v. Kendrick,* 527 F. Supp.

1252, 1310 (S.D. W. Va. 1981). Telephone access: *Moore v. Marketplace Restaurant, Inc.*, 754 F.2d 1336 (7th Cir. 1985); *Montana v. Commissioner's Court*, 659 F.2d 19 (5th Cir. 1981); *Inmates of Allegheny County Jail v. Wecht*, 565 F. Supp. 1278 (W.D. Pa. 1983); *Hearn v. Hudson*, 549 F. Supp. 949 (W.D. Va. 1982); *Wolfish v. Levi*, 439 F. Supp. 114 (S.D.N.Y. 1977).

XI
Parole

Parole has evolved over the past fifty years as an alternative to continued imprisonment: prisoners are selected for release and, theoretically, are provided with controls, assistance, and guidance to help them serve the remainder of their sentence in the free community. A large proportion of all prisoners in our correctional facilities will ordinarily be released on parole. Many others are eligible and are considered for release but are denied parole and serve their full sentence. The parole-granting process is, therefore, the most critical concern for the vast majority of all prisoners since it constitutes, in effect, a resentencing.[1]

In recent years there has been a movement to abolish or reduce reliance on parole as a release mechanism by the elimination of indeterminate sentencing. The current trend of having fixed sentence terms or mandatory minimum sentences does eliminate some of the abuses of the vast power given to parole authorities but, unfortunately, has resulted in harsher and longer sentences in many cases. This factor contributes to the severe overcrowding problems found across the nation.

When may a prisoner be released on parole?

Under most sentencing procedures, broad power is vested in the parole board to determine the length of an offender's term of imprisonment. Varying from jurisdiction to jurisdiction, a prisoner generally becomes eligible for parole when some part of his or her maximum term is served (one-third or one-half), or at the end of the minimum sentence. In some cases, the time may be reduced if the prisoner has earned good time or work-time credit, and—under some statutes—a prisoner may be eligible for parole as soon as the beginning of the term of imprisonment.

What is the procedure for granting parole?

Upon application by a prisoner for parole, institutional staff compile a case history of the applicant, based both on records available to the board and on information provided by the prisoner. The prisoner then goes before the parole board which evaluates all the records and ultimately decides on the parole application.

The decision to grant or deny parole is made in most cases on the basis of such factors as an offender's prior history, his or her readiness for release, institutional record, and need for supervision and assistance in the community prior to the expiration of the sentence. Typically, however, the decision as to whether parole should be granted is made on insufficient and often biased information. The information gathered by institutional officials about the parole applicant is usually compiled from meager and possibly inaccurate prison records, and often fits into a highly stereotyped format. Under current practices, the institutional report is often the decisive factor in a parole board's determination.

Parole for federal prisoners is currently handled by the United States Parole Commission which uses a system of parole release criteria in an effort to reduce the essentially arbitrary nature of parole decision making.[2] A prisoner's offense is scored as to its seriousness, and so-called "offender characteristics" such as prior record, drug use, education, family ties, parole plans, and institutional conduct are assigned a numerical score. These two factors, offense and offender characteristics, are then plotted on a chart to determine the prisoner's period of confinement prior to parole release.

This approach was replaced by the Sentencing Reform Act of 1984 (SRA)[3] which became effective 1 November 1987 (although the Parole Commission and current parole provisions will remain in effect for five years after the SRA becomes law). Under the SRA, the sentencing judge determines whether an additional term of supervised release will be added to the term of incarceration, according to guidelines that will be developed. Also under the SRA, probation officers will replace parole officers in supervising parolees. A violation of a condition of release may be construed as contempt of court, may result in the imposition of sanctions, and—if it is a new criminal law violation—may result in criminal prosecution. However, minor violations of supervised release will not be grounds for revocation. The SRA requires that serious violations should be addressed through additional criminal proceedings.

Do prisoners have any due process protections at parole release hearings?

In general, the answer is no. Hearings before the parole board are for the most part meaningless exercises. The prisoner is not represented by counsel or any other advisor, and he has no opportunity to present favorable information or to effectively rebut possibly damaging information. In effect, the prisoner merely has an interview with the board of parole or an individual member, which will rarely offer an effective opportunity for the prisoner to present any material that could affect the decision of the board. However, as a result of new federal parole statutes, federal prisoners are entitled to have an advisor represent them at the parole hearing, as well as to have some access to the information in their file and the opportunity to rebut damaging information, the right to present evidence at the parole hearing, the right to a transcript of the hearing, the right to a written result of the hearing with specific reasons for parole denial, and the right to appeal the decision.[4]

There had been substantial positive movement in the lower federal courts prior to 1979 with respect to procedural due process protections at parole release hearings. However, the Supreme Court, in *Greenholtz v. Inmates of the Nebraska Penal and Correctional Complex*,[5] cut back on that movement and held that the Due Process Clause by itself does not create any liberty or conditional liberty interest in obtaining parole and that absent any interest or entitlement created by state law, a prisoner was entitled to no procedural protections in the parole application process. The Court went on to say that Nebraska had created such an interest in its parole statutory scheme and that, therefore, prisoners were entitled to minimum due process. The Court held that the hearing and notice of decision furnished by the state parole board satisfied a prisoner's due process interest.[6]

As a result of *Greenholtz,* if a state has not created a liberty interest in parole, then the only due process protections to which a prisoner may be entitled may be those prescribed by state law. However, a parole board may not deny parole to a prisoner because of race,[7] religious prejudice,[8] national origin,[9] or poverty.[10] Nor may it be denied by considering an erroneous description of the conduct underlying an offense,[11] on the basis of an illegal disciplinary proceeding,[12] by the use of parole criteria which are vague and ambiguous,[13] or on the basis of an unconstitutional prison conviction.[14]

Most state statutes do not address the right to counsel at a parole hearing,[15] although counsel are permitted in many jurisdictions without specific statutory authority. Still fewer states provide counsel for indigent prisoners,[16] and the United States Supreme Court is unlikely to recognize such a right since it has failed to provide an across-the-board right to counsel at parole revocation or prison disciplinary hearings where it has found minimal due process rights.[17]

Are there restrictions on parolees?

Yes, the rights of persons on parole are greatly restricted. Typically, the parolee must report regularly to his or her parole officer, obtain permission to change residence or jobs or to get married, and the parolee must not have "questionable associates." In addition, many states restrict the parolee's right to travel and to speak freely, and they subject the parolee, his or her residence, and possessions to searches without a warrant. Failure to comply with any condition of parole may trigger parole revocation and a return to custody. And, of course, any conviction for a new crime while on parole will result in revocation. Approximately 35 percent of all those paroled are eventually returned to prison, and many of these parole violators are not returned for committing a new crime; rather, they are recommitted for violating a condition of parole. Thus, the nature of the conditions of parole are of the utmost significance.

Particular conditions of parole (and probation, which is similar in nature) have been subjected to challenge. In *Loving v. Commonwealth*,[18] banishment from a particular county was overturned; in *Sweeney v. United States*,[19] abstinence from drink for an alcoholic offender was overturned; and in *People v. Higgins*,[20] a condition of probation which prohibited a convicted burglar from playing college basketball was ruled invalid. The Supreme Court has ruled that the standard of "satisfactory evidence" of a parole violation before arrest is not met by proof that a parolee works at a night club which employs other ex-prisoners, when one parole condition was that he not "associate" with ex-prisoners.²¹ And a federal court has held that a parole condition which banned the "frequenting of bars" was unconstitutionally vague.²²

Do parolees have First Amendment rights?

Yes. Although courts have traditionally refused to interfere with the administrative rules and regulations of parole boards, in the First Amendment area they have abandoned the hands-off policy and have struck down arbitrary and unconstitutional parole regulations. In an important First Amendment case, a federal district court ruled that a United States Parole Board decision to restrict the right of Morton Sobell (on parole for espionage) to travel and speak at a dinner sponsored by a Communist party newspaper and to participate in antiwar demonstrations was unconstitutional.²³ The court held that the First Amendment rights of parolees may be limited only to serve valid penological purposes and ruled that there had been no showing of any public danger from Sobell's speech nor of any indication that his rehabilitation might be impaired. The court noted that totalitarian states use "rehabilitation" as a means of thought control and that rehabilitation is probably best approached by avoiding degrading and distrustful restrictions.

A California federal district court has similarly upheld the First Amendment rights of parolees in a case where a parolee was required to obtain permission from his parole officer before giving any public speech.²⁴ On two occasions, the parole officer refused the parolee permission to speak at colleges about conditions in the state's prisons, and the court found that on neither occasion had the parole officer shown a clear and present danger of riot or disorder. The court, therefore, enjoined the parole authorities from conditioning parole on a parolee's seeking advance permission to address public gatherings.

These cases were followed by the decision of the Tenth Circuit Court of Appeals which struck down parole conditions prohibiting a convicted income-tax violator from expressing his "fanatical" opinions about the constitutionality of the federal tax laws. The court held that the parolee had a constitutional right to express his opinions but could be prohibited from urging others to violate the law.²⁵

In contrast, in a probation case, the Ninth Circuit upheld a condition forbidding probationers who had been found guilty of illegally entering a submarine base from coming within 250 feet of the base.[26] Even though the court knew that the probationers would be unable to distribute literature to employees or attend meetings at a private location near the base, it did not find this restriction to violate rights of free speech and association. The court noted that the condition did not prevent all protest activity and that given the alternative of incarceration the limitation was reasonable.

Do parolees have a right to privacy?

The parolee's right to privacy is often circumscribed by parole regulations which permit parole officers to inspect a parolee's premises and possessions at any time without a search or arrest warrant. Obviously, arbitrary intrusions of privacy result from these restrictions on privacy, but most courts—stating that parole is both a privilege and a kind of custody—have held that the parolee cannot complain of Fourth Amendment violations when his or her right to privacy and personal autonomy is subject to arbitrary parole practices. In 1970, the Supreme Court of California held that in parole revocation proceedings, the Adult Authority could consider evidence that may have been seized in violation of the Fourth or Fifth Amendments although that evidence would be excluded at a criminal trial. The court limited the application of the exclusionary rule[27] to trials and stated that a parole agency, whose delicate duty is to decide when a convicted offender can be safely allowed to return and to remain in society, is in a different posture than the court, which decides initial guilt.[28]

Similarly, the Second Circuit Court of Appeals has ruled that the exclusionary rule should not apply at parole revocation hearings. The court stated that "a parole revocation proceeding is concerned not only with protecting society, but also, and most importantly, with rehabilitating and restoring to useful lives those placed in the custody of the parole board. To apply the exclusionary rule to parole revocation proceedings would tend to obstruct the parole system in accomplishing its remedial purposes."[29]

Some courts have established constitutional protections for the parolee. In one case, a federal district court in New York held that a parolee does not sacrifice his or her Fourth Amendment right to privacy by agreeing to be released on parole.

Law enforcement officials had illegally seized evidence from the parolee's residence and had started prosecution. The court suppressed the evidence, stating that a parolee cannot "generally be stripped of his constitutional rights, particularly since the effect of such a holding would be to expose him to self-incrimination and to surrender his privacy with respect to matters and offenses other than violation of parole."[30]

But, while the courts have generally held that parolees are entitled to Fourth Amendment protections, a parole officer with mere "reasonable suspicion" that a violation of law is occurring, rather than a constitutional requirement of "probable cause," can search a parolee's home, and the fruits of that search can be admitted at trial upon the new criminal charge.[31]

It seems apparent that at this point the courts are not willing to grant parolees that quantum of privacy that the Fourth Amendment guarantees to everyone else. However, arbitrary searches or invasions of privacy that are intended only to harass the parolee are not likely to pass muster even under the prevailing judicial standards.

For what reasons may parole be revoked?

Parole revocation proceedings may be instituted for any violation of the conditions of parole. Many revocations result from convictions for offenses committed while on parole. These are usually termed direct violations of parole and invariably result in a return to prison for the period of time that the parole was intended to cover. Thus, the prisoner who is released on ten years of parole will be recommitted on a direct violation to serve the entire ten years, even though the new offense may have been committed with only one year or six months left to the parole period.

A substantial number of revocations are the result of technical violations, that is, a violation of one or more of the conditions of parole. If revocation results under these circumstances, many states provide that the prisoner is entitled to credit for good "street time," thus limiting the new imprisonment to the time left on parole at the point of violation. This is now true for former federal prisoners on parole as a result of the 1976 changes in federal parole law.

Is a parolee entitled to any protections during the parole revocation process?

Yes. The United States Supreme Court, in *Morrissey v. Brewer*,[32] ruled that under the Fourteenth Amendment to the Constitution, parolees are entitled to minimum due process safeguards when their "conditional liberty" is threatened by an accusation that they have violated the conditions of parole. The Court outlined a two-step process. The first step involves a hearing to determine whether there is probable cause to believe that the parolee has committed the acts which constitute a violation of parole. This preliminary hearing must be conducted "reasonably near" the place where the alleged act occurred and as "promptly as convenient." The second stage involves a final determination of the relative facts with respect to the violation and whether or not these facts require revocation. The parolee would have an opportunity at this stage to present evidence that he or she did not violate the parole condition and could show circumstances in mitigation which might suggest that the violation does not warrant revocation.

At both stages, the Supreme Court outlined the minimum due process protections that the parolee would be entitled to. These protections include (1) written notice of the claimed violations; (2) disclosure to the parolee of the evidence against him; (3) opportunity to be heard in person and to present witnesses and documentary evidence; (4) the right to confront and cross-examine witnesses; (5) a neutral and detached hearing body; and (6) a written statement by the fact-finders as to the evidence relied on and the reasons for revoking parole.

In light of *Morrissey*, which held that due process mandated prompt revocation hearings, some courts held that a parolee subjected to a detainer had a right to a reasonably prompt execution of the detainer and subsequent revocation hearing. In *Moody v. Daggett*,[33] the Supreme Court addressed this split of authority and ruled that a federal parolee who had been convicted of another crime while on parole is not constitutionally entitled to a parole revocation hearing until he or she has fully served the sentence for the new crime. Post-*Moody* cases have rejected any distinction based on federal jurisdiction and have held that *Moody* applies irrespective of the jurisdiction involved.[34]

In another subsequent Supreme Court decision, *Gagnon v. Scarpelli*,[35] the Court established a limited right to representation of counsel during this process when a request is made on the basis that the parolee did not commit the violation or there were substantial or complex reasons justifying or mitigating the violation. In addition, there must be some indication that the parolee cannot speak effectively for him- or herself. When *Gagnon* does not apply, the indigent parolee must look to rights under state law.[36]

NOTES

1. A good treatise on this subject is Cohen and Gobert, *Law of Probation and Parole* (Shepard's/McGraw-Hill, 1983). *Also see* annual pocketparts.
2. Parole Commission and Reorganization Act of 1975, 18 U.S.C. §§ 4201–18.
3. Pub. L. No. 98-473, 98 stat. 1987 (1984).
4. *Supra* note 1.
5. 442 U.S. 1, 99 S. Ct. 2100, 60 L. Ed. 2d 668 (1979). See also *Bd. of Pardons v. Allen*, __U.S.__, 107 S. Ct. 2415, __L. Ed. 2d__ (1987).
6. *Greenholtz*, 442 U.S. at 16.
7. *Block v. Potter*, 631 F.2d 233 (3d Cir. 1980).
8. *Farries v. U.S. Bd. of Parole*, 484 F.2d 948 (7th Cir. 1973).
9. *Texas Supporters of Workers World Presidential Candidates v. Strake*, 511 F. Supp. 149 (S.D. Tex. 1981).
10. *See Cruz v. Skelton*, 543 F.2d 86 (5th Cir. 1976).
11. *Kohlman v. Norton*, 380 F. Supp. 1073 (D. Conn. 1974).
12. *Leonard v. Mississippi State Probation and Parole Bd.*, 373 F. Supp. 699 (N.D. Miss. 1974).
13. *Billiteri v. U.S. Bd. of Parole*, 385 F. Supp. 1217 (W.D.N.Y. 1974).
14. *Sammons v. Rodgers*, 785 F.2d 1343 (5th Cir. 1986).
15. *But see, e.g.*, Hawaii Rev. Stat. § 706-670(2); Neb. Rev. Stat. § 83-1, 112(2); S.C. Code Ann. § 24-21-50 (Law Co-op); Vt. Stat. Ann. § 502(b).
16. *See, e.g.*, Hawaii Rev. Stat. § 706-670(2).
17. *See Morrissey v. Brewer*, 408 U.S. 471, 92 S. Ct. 2593, 33 L. Ed. 2d 484 (1972) and *Wolff v. McDonnell*, 418 U.S. 539, 94 S. Ct. 2963, 41 L. Ed. 2d 935 (1974).
18. 206 Va. 924, 147 S.E.2d 78 (Va. 1966).
19. 353 F.2d 10 (7th Cir. 1965).
20. 22 Mich. App. 479, 177 N.W.2d 716 (1970).
21. *Arciniega v. Freeman*, 404 U.S. 4, 92 S. Ct. 22, 30 L. Ed. 2d 126 (1971).
22. *Panko v. McCauley*, 473 F. Supp. 325 (E.D. Wis. 1979).

23. *Sobell v. Reed,* 327 F.Supp 1294 (S.D.N.Y. 1971). *But see Berrigan v. Sigler,* 499 F.2d 514 (D.C. Cir. 1974)(restriction on overseas travel upheld).

24. *Hyland v. Procunier,* 311 F. Supp. 749 (N.D. Cal. 1970).

25. *Porth v. Templar,* 453 F.2d 330 (10th Cir. 1971).

26. *United States v. Lowe,* 654 F.2d 562 (9th Cir. 1981).

27. The exclusionary rule refers to that method used by courts to exclude from criminal proceedings any evidence (such as confession or contraband) obtained by law enforcement officials in violation of the defendant's constitutional rights.

28. *In re Martinez,* 1 Cal. 3d 641, 463 P.2d 734, 83 Cal. Rptr. 382 (Cal. 1970).

29. *United States ex rel. Sperling v. Fitzpatrick,* 426 F.2d 1161 (2d Cir. 1970).

30. *United States v. Lewis,* 274 F. Supp. 184, 190 (S.D.N.Y. 1967).

31. *Latta v. Fitzharris,* 521 F.2d 246 (9th Cir. 1975) and *United States v. Smith,* 395 F. Supp. 1155 (W.D.N.Y. 1975).

32. *See Morrissey v. Brewer, supra* note 17.

33. 429 U.S. 78, 97 S. Ct. 274, 50 L. Ed. 2d 236 (1976).

34. *See, e.g., United States ex rel. Sims v. Sielaff,* 563 F.2d 821 (7th Cir. 1977).

35. 411 U.S. 778, 93 S. Ct. 1756, 36 L. Ed. 2d 656 (1973).

36. Hawaii Rev. Stat. § 706-670(2)(c); Pa. Stat. Ann. Tit. 37, § 71.4(3); *People ex rel. Donahoe v. Montanye,* 35 N.Y.2d 221, 318 N.E.2d 781, 360 N.Y.S.2d 619 (1974).

XII

Remedies and Procedures for Challenging Conditions of Confinement

As reflected in previous chapters, the constitutional rights of prisoners are few and narrowly defined. Federal court archives and dead case storage cabinets are cluttered with the paper remains of an endless succession of prisoner conditions cases that failed because the cases did not fall within the limited scope of the Constitution's coverage. While far-reaching successes in some federal litigation over the past two decades evidence the fact that inmates are not entirely stripped of their constitutional rights and that the Constitution does not stop at the prison gate,[1] the fact that few of the thousands of prisoner cases brought each year in the federal courts even survive the initial reading of the complaint demonstrates that inmates must begin to consider alternatives to federal court litigation, options that may take them down roads they have avoided in the past.

This chapter will identify forums in addition to federal courts where relief from oppressive or hostile institutional conditions can be obtained by prisoners, focus on how to decide where to pursue such relief, and discuss in a general way how to proceed in federal court after the decision to file suit there has been made.

Are there any administrative procedures available for the review of prisoner complaints?

Yes. Most prison systems have internal grievance programs which permit inmates to register complaints about conditions or practices within the institution. While the formats and procedures of these programs vary from system to system, most programs enable prisoners to submit written complaints to a designated complaint officer on a range of matters related to conditions of confinement such as the quality of medical care, abuse by guards and other personnel, correspondence rights, transfers to other institutions, and the loss of privileges. The complaint officer renders a decision—usually an informal, written response—which may or may not be appealable to a higher official such as the warden or deputy warden.

There are factors operating within prison environments that raise serious questions from the prisoner's standpoint about the fairness or effectiveness of such programs. Inmates are routinely relegated to second-class status; their credibility is greatly devalued. Guards and prison administrators often strive to present a united front. Under these circumstances, it is unlikely that prison officials will change general policy, decide in favor of an individual in response to an inmate complaint, or reverse negative decisions made by lower level personnel. These programs—at the very least—lack even the appearance of fairness. In addition, most programs do not have an in-depth, fact-finding process, and statements secured from prison personnel are not routinely given under oath or subject to cross-examination. To a large extent, the quality of the programs depend upon the integrity and work habits of the complaint officer and his willingness to take an aggressive or unpopular stand on behalf of inmates.

Despite these negative factors, there are reasons for pursuing an administrative grievance before or instead of filing a lawsuit. One reason is that it is usually much easier to file and prosecute a grievance than to prepare an adequate lawsuit. Prison administrative procedures are not encumbered by the complexities found in court systems. No particular skills or knowledge on the inmate's part are required to prosecute grievances. Moreover, administrative decisions are ordinarily rendered much sooner than judicial decisions, which are slowed by the high volume of cases that clog the court dockets as well as the dilatory maneuvers of defense counsel. A second reason is that even a bad grievance system sometimes makes a favorable decision.

Third, in a handful of prison systems, exhaustion of administrative procedures is required before resorting to the federal courts under a provision of the Civil Rights of Institutionalized Persons Act (CRIPA).[2] Some state court systems also require exhaustion of prison administrative procedures before suit in state court can be filed.

Pursuing administrative remedies may also produce a public relations benefit for the prisoner. Many judges believe that most prisoner claims do not really belong in court and that prisoners use the courts to annoy prison officials or to disrupt the court system. By first resorting to the prison's internal grievance program, a prisoner's lawsuit may receive a more sympathetic reception since it indicates that the inmate acted reasonably by attempting to resolve the problem within prison channels. Still another advantage of resorting first to administrative processes is that it sometimes produces information or statements from prison officials that can be accumulated as evidence and used subsequently in court. But perhaps the most pressing reason for using internal grievance programs is that in many cases the prisoner has no real choice but to do so. There are numerous conditions and practices within prisons that—while harsh, unreasonable, or unfair—are not illegal under state or federal law. For such cases, it would be futile to file a lawsuit. The only realistic option available under these circumstances is to vigorously pursue a grievance within the institutional program and hope for the best.

What other forums are available for the review of prisoners' complaints?

There are two judicial systems available to hear and decide inmate complaints: the state court system and the federal court system. Because federal courts have historically been much more receptive to prisoner rights complaints than state courts, the overwhelming number of lawsuits filed by prisoners to challenge institutional conditions and practices over the past two decades have been initiated in federal district courts. While the relative receptiveness of the two systems still tilts in the direction of the federal courts, in recent years the federal system has become less receptive to inmate civil rights actions while an increasing number of state courts have become more responsive to inmate cases. As a result, decision as to the best forum in which to initiate suit is now less obvious than it once was and is not one that should be made without some serious consideration.

When choosing between a state or federal forum, perhaps the most important factor for a prisoner to keep in mind is that federal courts have no jurisdiction to hear prison-related cases that solely involve violations of state law.[3] Access to the federal courts by state or local prisoners is primarily made possible by the Federal Civil Rights Act of 1871, a statute which makes it unlawful for state or local officials to deprive any person of a right, privilege, or immunity secured by the federal Constitution or statutes.[4] A case of prison officials violating an aspect of state law does *not* amount to a federal civil rights violation, and the federal courts are powerless to hear the case. Therefore, in the absence of some reason to believe that federal constitutional rights have been violated, it makes little sense to initiate suit in the federal court system since the case is likely to be dismissed or lost at some point in the litigation. In light of this condition, when determining **where** to file suit, an inmate should attempt as best he can to determine whether a viable federal claim exists or whether the wrongdoing involves no more than a violation of state law. If the latter is true, a federal suit should be ruled out.

Even when a federal right has been infringed, serious consideration should be given to filing suit in a local state court, unless there is reason to believe that the judges in the local system are less receptive to prison conditions complaints than the federal judges in that region. As alluded to previously, state courts have responded affirmatively to complaints in many areas where overcrowding and oppressive conditions prevail. In some cases they have relied on the federal Constitution as the basis for relief. However, in others they have relied upon the state Constitution, state or local health and safety code statutes, prison regulations, and other such bases which sometimes go further than the federal Constitution in protecting inmates and regulating prison conditions.

On the other hand, there are positive factors pointing in the direction of federal court—when a federal right is involved. Among other things, federal judges are ordinarily more familiar with constitutional principles and more accustomed to applying the Civil Rights Act than are state judges. In addition, federal judges are insulated or further removed from the pressures of local politics, a consideration that has particular pertinence to cases involving unpopular or inflammatory issues or the potential expenditure of large sums of tax dollars.

If a prisoner decides to file suit in the federal court system, must the prison's administrative complaint procedures be exhausted before doing so or should a state court be given the opportunity to first decide the case?

As indicated previously, most claims by prisoners in the federal court system proceed on the basis of the Civil Rights

Act of 1871, more commonly referred to as Section 1983. Section 1983 suits do not require exhaustion of state remedies.[5] Therefore, prisoners are not required to apply for relief to prison administrators nor to the state courts before serving in federal court for a violation of civil rights.

However, there is one limited exception to the no-exhaustion principle in prison conditions suits, an exception found in CRIPA, mentioned earlier in this chapter. The act authorizes federal district courts to continue or suspend activity on a civil rights case for up to ninety days in order to require inmates to exhaust prison administrative remedies if the prison complaint program meets minimum standards of fairness and if exhaustion in that particular case would be appropriate and in the interest of justice. However, exhaustion is only required where the United States attorney general has certified the grievance process or the district court finds that it conforms to a series of requirements specified in the statute and implementing regulations. The requirements include, among other things, an advisory role for inmates in the formulation, implementation, and operation of the program and a provision for independent review of the disposition of grievances by a person not under the direct supervision or control of the institution. However, since few grievance programs conform to the minimum requirements of the act, this limited exhaustion requirement is rarely applicable and in most instances represents no barrier to the immediate prosecution of a federal civil rights lawsuit.

What relief may a prisoner request in suits commenced under the Civil Rights Act?

Prisoners proceeding under the Civil Rights Act have the full range of relief available to them that other plaintiffs have under the act. Depending upon the nature of the case, they may seek declaratory or injunctive relief as well as money damages.

What is declaratory relief and when should it be requested?

A declaratory judgment is a means by which a party may obtain a binding declaration regarding his rights.[6] The Federal Declaratory Judgment Act provides that in a case or "actual controversy within its jurisdiction," a federal court "may declare

the rights and other legal relations of any interested party
seeking such declaration, whether or not further relief is or
could be sought." A declaratory judgment, in itself, does not
abate the conditions or priorities complained about or require
compensation for a plaintiff's injuries or losses. It is not an
order mandating that somebody act or refrain from acting.
Instead, it serves to declare whether a legal obligation exists
between the plaintiff and defendants, essentially operating as
a recognition by the court that the plaintiff's rights have been
violated and as a prelude for additional relief in the form of
damages or an injunction. Therefore, declaratory judgments
are usually routinely requested in a complaint in conjunction
with a request for an injunction and/or money damages.

What is an injunction and when should a prisoner seek one?
An injunction is a court order either prohibiting a party from
engaging in a specific course of activity or requiring a party to
perform some action. It is a remedy that should be requested
when a prisoner is being subjected to or imminently threatened
by unconstitutional conditions or practices and wishes to have
the conditions or practices stopped or changed. Injunctive relief
has been the primary vehicle by which prisoners have succeeded in terminating a broad array of unconstitutional matters
within prison walls.

When is a request for money damages appropriate?
Three categories of damages are available in civil rights prisoner cases: compensatory, nominal, and punitive damages.
Whether any or all categories of damages are available in a
given case depends, of course, on the particular facts of the
case.

1. Compensatory Damages. The basic purpose of damages
under Section 1983 is to compensate persons for injuries that
were caused by the deprivation of their constitutional rights.[7]
Compensatory damages, therefore, are recoverable under the
act only if the plaintiff can prove that the denial of a constitutional right has actually injured him.[8] No compensatory damages can be awarded for the violation of a constitutional right
in the absence of proof of actual injury.[9] The Supreme Court
has recently held that injuries do not flow from the "abstract
value" or importance of the constitutional right infringed.[10]
Instead, they flow from the harm caused by the violation.

Compensatory damages may include not only out-of-pocket losses and other monetary harms, but also less concrete losses such as mental and emotional distress, emotional pain and suffering, and personal humiliation. Therefore, when a prisoner has been injured or harmed as a result of the violation of his constitutional rights, a request for compensatory damages is a proper remedy to pursue.

Due to a variety of factors, most damage awards in prison cases are relatively small. Large awards are generally limited to cases involving serious bodily harm or gross mistreatment. Therefore, when requesting damages in the complaint or during settlement discussions (should they occur) the amount of damages sought should not be set at an unrealistically high level. Asking for enormous sums of money may antagonize the court or cause it not to take the case seriously. It may also discourage defendants from making a settlement offer.

2. *Nominal Damages.* Nominal damages in the amount of one dollar or some similar token amount are recoverable for at least some constitutional violations where no actual injuries were produced by the violation. This is because the law recognizes the importance to society of certain "absolute" rights and the need to have such rights scrupulously observed. In light of this fact, a request for nominal damages can either be made by itself or in conjunction with a request for compensatory and/or punitive damages where either the existence of actual injury or the ability to prove actual injury is doubtful.

3. *Punitive Damages.* Punitive or exemplary damages are available in a Section 1983 case when the defendants' conduct is "shown to be motivated by evil motive or intent, or when it involves reckless or callous indifference to the federally protected rights of others."[11] The purpose of awarding such damages is to punish the defendants for their conduct or to deter them and others from committing similar acts in the future.[12] They are available whether or not actual damages have been proven and may be awarded where only nominal damages had been established.[13]

Punitive damages are rarely granted, even in cases where the court awards compensatory damages. While it would not be inappropriate to request them when there is reason to believe that defendants' conduct was motivated by malicious purposes or by needless or callous indifference to the inmate's constitutional rights, it would be unrealistic to expect to recover punitive damages except in the most shocking or outrageous factual circumstances.

Are there any legal barriers to the recovery of money damages in Section 1983 prison conditions suits?

There is one prominent barrier to the recovery of money damages that state prisoners often face when pursuing Section 1983 conditions claims. The Supreme Court has held that government officials and employees are entitled to "qualified immunity" from money judgments.[14] Under the qualified immunity doctrine, officials are liable for damages only if they "know or should have known" they were violating the plaintiff's rights—that is, only if they were violating "clearly established statutory or constitutional rights of which a reasonable person would have known" at the times the acts were committed.[15] While persons occupying public positions are expected to have knowledge of the basic unquestioned constitutional rights of their charges,[16] they are not required "to be aware of a constitutional right that has not yet been declared."[17]

Therefore, a potential issue in all damage claims against prison personnel is whether they knew or should have known they were violating the prisoner's constitutional rights. In many areas (medical care, environmental conditions, disciplinary procedures, etc.), the conditional obligation of prison personnel to inmates has been clearly established, and the question of whether the official is immune from suit will not be a serious one even if raised by the defendant. In other, less clear-cut cases, the courts will have to review the case law to determine whether the right allegedly violated was clearly established at the time of the alleged misconduct. In any event, the defense of qualified governmental immunity is applicable to the question of damages and will not bar a request for injunctive relief.[18]

Is it necessary for prisoners challenging prison conditions in federal court to be represented by attorneys?

Prisoners have a right to represent themselves. This is known as proceeding *pro se*. But while having legal counsel is not mandatory, it is usually important. Representation by an attorney often assures that the various tasks required in civil rights litigation are handled properly and efficiently. Even when a prisoner is familiar with the applicable legal principles, attorneys are usually in a better position to handle the difficult tasks of litigation by virtue of their experience and the fact that they are not locked away in defendants' custody. Representation by counsel often increases the likelihood that the case will be heard and decided more quickly. Pretrial discovery will usually proceed more smoothly, the preparation of briefs will often be more thorough, and the opportunity for an effective trial will be enhanced by the presence of counsel. *Pro se* suits are often taken less seriously by the courts than lawyer-assisted cases, and the chance that a *pro se* case will be lost among the volumes of *pro se* cases filed each year is not remote. Nonetheless, despite the obvious benefits of having attorneys assist them, prisoners are usually unable to secure counsel for civil rights cases. While the Sixth Amendment guarantees a criminal defendant the right to counsel, there is no right to counsel in civil prison conditions suits.

Prisoners who are indigent and lack the financial resources to file civil rights cases and retain counsel are authorized by federal statute to apply for permission to proceed in *forma pauperis* and to request appointment of an attorney.[19] Under the statute, the court does not have the authorepresentation.[10] The court merely has the discretion to "*request* that an attorney represent [a] person unable to employ counsel. . . ."[21]

Some of the factors considered by federal courts when determining whether to request counsel are whether the case appears to have much chance of success;[20] whether the prisoner is in a position to investigate the crucial facts needed to establish his claims;[23] whether there are facts in dispute and whether they are complicated and require substantial cross-examination;[24] the complexity of the legal issues raised in the case and whether the law is unclear;[25] and whether the plaintiff has the capacity to present the case himself.[26] In some jurisdictions, federal courts have access to panels of volunteer attorneys to whom requests can be made, or they will attempt to obtain counsel through legal aid programs and other similar organizations. However, it is a rare instance when a court will make such a request either because of a shortage of volunteer attorneys available for such assignments in the jurisdiction or because the court determines that factors indicating the need for counsel are not present in the case.

Since assignment of counsel generally does not occur, prisoners—except in the most compelling and complex cases—should probably focus their efforts to obtain legal assistance on their own, either by contacting a local legal aid program or some other agency that handles prison conditions cases or, if that fails, by seeking assistance from skilled jailhouse lawyers with whom they have a constitutional right to consult.[27]

How is a Section 1983 action initiated in federal court by a prisoner who is representing her- or himself?

A claim based on the Civil Rights Act must begin with the filing of a complaint in the district court where the claim arose or where all the defendants reside. Ordinarily, this is the district court closest to the prison where the conditions or events giving rise to the action took place.

A complaint, which may be handwritten, is the document in which the prisoner first informs the court about the facts that have caused or lead to the violation of the prisoner's constitutional rights. It should be a simple, straightforward, and complete story—from beginning to end—of how and when the plaintiff's constitutional rights were violated, who was responsible for the violation, and how the plaintiff was harmed by the conditions or practices under complaint. The factual accounting should not be told in stilted, formal, legalistic language but in simple terms that can be clearly understood by the court. The complaint cannot be a document with little or no facts. It cannot be a narration constructed from unsupported conclusions—such as "I didn't receive adequate medical care for my illness," or "they didn't give me enough exercise time while I was in solitary confinement." Although complaints by *pro se* prisoners will be read with a more lenient eye than attorney-drafted complaints,[28] they must contain at least a minimum number of facts to support such conclusions if they are to avoid an early dismissal.[29] Therefore in the above medical example, the complaints should have described—among other things—the nature of the illness, the nature of the care provided, the physical or emotional consequences produced by the absence of adequate care, the time period the complaint involves, and the persons who were responsible for the prisoner not receiving care. When complaining about the lack of exercise, the solitary confinement prisoner should have related, among other things, the length of time in solitary confinement, general conditions within the cell, the number of hours confined to the cell, how much time was allowed for out-of-cell exercise, the physical or emotional consequences produced by the lack of recreation, and the names and positions of the persons who were responsible for the deprivation.

A *pro se* complaint does not have to specify the constitutional right that was infringed, since *pro se* prisoners—unlike attorneys—are not required to be learned in the law. However, if a prisoner suspects that a particular constitutional amendment was violated in the case, it is helpful to identify the right in the pleading since it helps to direct the court to the nature of the complaint.

The complaint should identify each of the defendants by name and position and should factually describe their actions or how they were otherwise involved in the constitutional infringement.

After describing how the constitutional rights were or are being violated and identifying each defendant responsible for the violation, a complaint should specify the nature of the relief the plaintiff wishes the court to grant. As outlined earlier in this chapter, the relief requested can include an award of money damages, an injunction, or a declaratory judgment or some combination of these remedies depending upon the facts of the particular case.

Complaint forms for *pro se* cases are furnished by most, if not all, district courts in this country and may be obtained from the clerk of courts. In some districts, the clerk of the court will accept only complaints written on the forms.

The filing of a complaint in federal court ordinarily must be accompanied by a filing fee. However, persons who are too poor to pay a filing fee may—with court approval—file without prepayment of fees under the authority of the federal *forma pauperis* statute.[30]

What happens after a complaint has been filed?

The court will review a *pro se* complaint that is proceeding in *forma pauperis* to determine whether it is "frivolous." If so, the complaint will not be served on the defendants. If the complaint is not deemed to be frivolous, service will be ordered—at no cost to the plaintiff—and the case begins its journey toward resolution.

Often, defendants will move to dismiss the case—arguing that even if the facts are as the plaintiff alleges, either no constitutional violation has occurred or plaintiff is not entitled to any relief against them.[31] An overwhelming number of cases filed by inmates are dismissed in this fashion—often because the complaint is too vague, a constitutional infringement has not occurred, or the wrong parties have been sued. The plaintiff, of course, has a right to present written arguments against a dismissal and often is permitted to amend the complaint to cure the defects cited by defendants. Assuming no motion to dismiss is filed in the case or the complaint survives a motion to dismiss, the plaintiff is permitted by the Federal Rules of Civil Procedure to engage in discovery. Through interrogatories (written questions addressed to the defendants), requests for production of documents, and other discovery tools, the plaintiff can attempt to uncover the information and documents needed to establish a case.[32] Many courts are careful to limit what they perceive to be routine inmate abuses of the discovery process, such as asking too many or irrelevant questions in interrogatories or requesting documents that have nothing conceivable to do with the case.

At the conclusion of the discovery period, either party may move for summary judgment—a procedure which permits the court to decide a case on the discovery materials, written affidavits, and other documents when the important facts are not in dispute. Assuming no summary judgment motion is filed—or if it is denied by the court—the case eventually goes to trial.

NOTES

1. *See Wolff v. McDonnell*, 418 U.S. 539, 94 S. Ct. 2963, 41 L. Ed. 2d 935 (1974).
2. 42 U.S.C. § 1997e.
3. *See* 28 U.S.C. § 1343(3), the normal jurisdictional basis for prison conditions complaints. It limits jurisdiction to deprivations under color of state law of rights, privileges, and immunities secured by the federal Constitution and acts of Congress.

4. 42 U.S.C. § 1983.
5. *Monroe v. Pape*, 365 U.S. 167, 81 S. Ct. 473, 5 L. Ed. 2d 492 and *Patsy v. Bd. of Regents of State of Fla.*, 457 U.S. 496, 102 S. Ct. 2557, 73 L. Ed. 2d 172 (1982).
6. 28 U.S.C. §§ 2201-2.
7. *Memphis Community School Dist. v. Stachura*, __U.S.__, 106 S. Ct. 2537, 2543, 91 L. Ed. 2d 265 (1986).
8. *Carey v. Piphus*, 435 U.S. 247, 254, 98 S. Ct. 1042, 55 L. Ed. 2d 252 (1978).
9. *Id.* at 264.
10. *Memphis Community School Dist. v. Stachura, supra*, at 2546.
11. *Smith v. Wade*, 461 U.S. 30, 56, 103 S. Ct. 1625, 75 L. Ed. 2d 632 (1983).
12. *Id.* at 54.
13. *Spence v. Staras*, 507 F.2d 554, 558 (7th Cir. 1974) and *Basista v. Weir*, 340 F.2d 74, 86–88 (3d Cir. 1965).
14. *See Harlow v. Fitzgerald*, 457 U.S. 800, 815, 102 S. Ct. 2727, 73 L. Ed. 2d 396 (1982).
15. *Harlow v. Fitzgerald, supra*, at 818.
16. *Wood v. Strickland*, 420 U.S. 308, 321-22, 95 S. Ct. 992, 43 L. Ed. 2d 214 (1975).
17. *Procunier v. Navarette*, 434 U.S. 555, 565, 98 S. Ct. 855, 55 L. Ed. 2d 24 (1978).
18. *National Treasury Employees Union v. Nixon*, 492 F.2d 587 (D.C. Cir. 1974) and *Knell v. Bensinger*, 522 F.2d 720 (7th Cir. 1975).
19. *See* 28 U.S.C. § 1915(d).
20. An attorney who wins a civil rights case on behalf of a prisoner can petition for fees at the conclusion of the case. However the entitlement to a fee depends on prevailing in the suit and the amount of recovery—which is to be paid by the defendants—is determined by the court. *See* 42 U.S.C. § 1988. Also *Hensley v. Eckerhart*, 461 U.S. 424, 103 S. Ct. 1933, 76 L. Ed. 2d 40 (1983).
21. 28 U.S.C. § 1915(d).
22. *See Mosby v. Mabry*, 697 F.2d 213 (8th Cir. 1982).
23. *See Slavin v. Curry*, 690 F.2d 446 (5th Cir. 1982) and *Stringer v. Rowe*, 616 F.2d 993 (7th Cir. 1980).
24. *See Lopez v. Reyes*, 692 F.2d 15 (5th Cir. 1982).
25. *See Merritt v. Faulkner*, 697 F.2d 761 (7th Cir. 1983).
26. *See Gordon v. Leake*, 574 F.2d 1147, 1153 (4th Cir. 1978) and *Drone v. Hutto*, 565 F.2d 543 (8th Cir. 1977).
27. *See Johnson v. Avery*, 393 U.S. 483, 89 S. Ct. 747, 21 L. Ed. 2d. 718 (1969), *rev'd and remanded*, 382 F.2d 353 (6th Cir. 1967).
28. *Haines v. Kerner*, 404 U.S. 519, 520–21, 92 S. Ct. 594, 30 L. Ed. 2d

652 (1972). *Also see Hughes v. Rowe,* 449 U.S. 5, 101 S. Ct. 173, 66 L. Ed. 2d 163 (1980).

29. *See Gray v. Creamer,* 465 F.2d 179, 182, n.2 (3d Cir. 1972).
30. 28 U.S.C. § 1915(a).
31. *See* Rule 12(b)(6) of the Federal Rules of Civil Procedure.
32. *See* Rules 26–34, of the Federal Rules of Civil Procedure.

Appendix

Prisoners' Rights Organizations

The following national organizations are active in prisoners' rights litigation:

National Prison Project of the ACLU Foundation, Inc.
1616 P Street, N.W., Suite 340
Washington, DC 20036

The NAACP Legal Defense Fund
99 Hudson Street, 10th Floor
New York, NY 10013

Southern Prisoners' Defense Committee, Inc.
185 Walton Street
Atlanta GA 30303

Selected Bibliography

Legal Rights of Prisoners, G. Alpert (Sage Publications, 1980).

The National Prison Project Journal, The National Prison Project of the ACLU Foundation (Quarterly).

Primer for Jail Litigators, 1st Ed., The National Prison Project of the ACLU Foundation (1984).

Prisoners and the Law, I. Robbins, ed., (Clark Boardman Company, 1985).

Prisoners Self-Help Litigation Manual, D. Manville and J. Boston, (Oceana Publications, Inc., 1983).

Rights of Prisoners, N. Cohen and J. Gobert (Shepard's/McGraw-Hill, 1981) and annual pocketparts.